TOTAL CUSTOMER FOCUS

TOTAL CUSTOMER FOCUS

The Roadmap to
Sustainable Profitability

Chris J. Stern

Copyright © 2004 by Chris J. Stern.

Library of Congress Number:		2004097133
ISBN:	Hardcover	1-4134-6809-8
	Softcover	1-4134-6808-X

All rights reserved. No part of this book may be reproduced or transmitted in any form or by any means, electronic or mechanical, including photocopying, recording, or by any information storage and retrieval system, without permission in writing from the copyright owner.

This book was printed in the United States of America.

To order additional copies of this book, contact:
Xlibris Corporation
1-888-795-4274
www.Xlibris.com
Orders@Xlibris.com

CONTENTS

PREFACE 9
PURSUE THE WOW 11
FOCUS ON ENTERPRISE VALUE ADDED 23
KNOW YOUR UNCERTAINTY 30
TAKE YOUR SHOT 39
ARE YOU "EASY TO DO BUSINESS WITH"? 56
TOP OF MIND 60
JUST DO IT 68
CHANGE 95
ONE-PAGE SUMMARY 101
INDEX 103
ENDNOTES 109

DEDICATION

My thanks go to Eva, Raphael and Deborah.
You are the people who made this book possible.

A special dedication goes to
my clients and students.
I could not have done the research
required and built the business tools in
this book, without your cooperation

PREFACE

This book describes a concept of how one can outperform competition in a global economy with total customer focus. Outperformance takes place when above-average leadership qualities within an organization stimulate the employees and stakeholders of a company to achieve results that could not be achieved with a generic strategy. The ideas presented in this book reflect the contributions of many brilliant individuals, and my humble added value is in combining them into a down-to-earth tool set for management. The idea of using tool sets and charts to memorize and visualize methodology came up during my consulting practice when I worked with tools and sets that were too complicated to implement without the help of a consultant. Of course, this may be exactly what certain larger consultancies want their clients to experience. In my terminology we call these "confusograms." My clients, however, were mostly small and medium-size companies that were indifferent to the latest management fads—they expected immediate results. I have been a senior executive in many positions before becoming a consultant and teacher, and I therefore know what results executives and managers expect. As a consequent step in my career, I founded my own institute and consultancy in Bonita Springs, Florida, in 1998. It is my objective to promote stringent and simple processes in strategy development and to empower readers to do their own long—and midterm planning processes. I am incorporating many practical examples, templates, and explanations for every tool shown. It is important to know that the processes promoted are very flexible; if you do not agree with the use of a certain tool, or if you feel that you do not need it, just skip it or add another one that is more appropriate for your specific situation. What is important is that you come up with your own best practice process and constantly improve it. Business administration is more of an art than a science; it is experience and innovation utilized effectively. There are certain rules that can guide you, but there is no such thing as "right or wrong" in business. Everyone can make up new business administration rules just by applying new ideas. Sir Richard Branson did so with Virgin Atlantic Airways, Hasso Plattner did so with SAP, and Michael Dell did so with Dell Computers. If any of these pioneers had followed the business administration rules of their time, they would never have started their businesses. What I am presenting to you has been proven many times, and it works.

Bonita Springs, July 2004

PURSUE THE WOW

In 1994, management guru Tom Peters wrote a book entitled *The Pursuit of Wow!*.[1] I truly believe that you must create products and services possessing a "wow" of some kind. "Wow" refers to unexpected excellence or performance. The kinds of "wow" you are able to create in products or services are related to a clear definition of the business you are in and your competitive position within that business. What kind of relationship do you have to a product or to a company providing a service before you experience the crucial "wow" moment? In most cases, there is no relationship at all, because you received a commodity. If you get something that is clearly better than expected, the "wow" comes over your lips easily.

I was flying from Miami, Florida, to Zurich, Switzerland, on a Swissair plane in January 2002. The flight was nothing spectacular, besides the fact that Swissair was broke and operated under the Swiss liquidation law (similar to chapter 11 bankruptcy). The new airline Swiss[2] was not yet born, and no employee knew whether they would have a job in April or not. The Airbus 330 left Miami late and was not able to make up the delay. However, scheduled within five minutes of the new arrival time, I had a connecting flight from Zurich via

Munich to Graz. You all know the feeling when your plane is still approaching the runway and you should already be at the connecting gate. Finally, we got into Zurich, and the plane was parked at the farthest gate available. I already imagined myself waiting at the service desk, calling my client to reschedule all appointments, and ultimately losing half a day of billings due to this delay. Of course, all this happened with the aching fatigue of a transatlantic flight in my bones. When the jetway was docked, I intended to storm out of the plane in order to reorganize. Right there, at the gate, was an elegant lady in uniform holding a sign with my name; Madeleine Kummer of Swissair VIP Services was waiting for me. "We are a little bit late for your Munich flight, which is actually scheduled to board within five minutes, Mr. Stern," she said politely (as if I had not been aware of this before) with a Swiss-Dutch accent, "but we will see what we can do." We walked to the closest terminal instead of heading to the Munich gate. "No time," Madeleine remarked and led me through the closest security gate she could find. Immediately after this, we went down the stairways to the tarmac and got into a limo. We drove to the outside field where the Munich plane was waiting, getting there just as the bus with all the other passengers arrived. Via radio, Ms. Kummer checked me in, and I safely made all remaining connections of the day. That is service as it should be. Could it have been different? Certainly, considering that the motivation of employees in a bankrupt company is at its lowest point. This brought me to the measurement factor of "wow": When was the last time you sent a thank you note for extraordinary services, or even flowers or candies to one of your suppliers? "Wows" are about people who go that extra mile to make a common product or service superb. Like Tom Peters said long ago, "wow" needs to be pursued. A key element in creating differentiation is knowing what kind of business you are in and what your strategic control point within this business is. The strategic control point indicates the percentage of the value chain you really control or at least significantly influence. The higher your strategic control point, the better you are positioned to create uniqueness and extramile services. It does not matter at all what size your organization is, as long as you behave according to your size. When Sir Richard Branson was asked what he does in the air transportation business, he replied that foremost he was not in air transportation, but rather in the entertainment business at thirty thousand feet in the air. Clue: He does not have the largest airline, or the best network in alliances—he is just entertaining his passengers much better than any other airline in the world. Doing so at thirty thousand feet has the advantage that passengers cannot escape the temptations ranging from incredible duty-free offerings, latest pay-per-view movies, and thousands of music titles. His business definition leads him to actually be the benchmark in entertained aviation.

If you are in a product-centered business, you want to be in the position where your customers actually bid just to get your goods. Unfortunately, only a few suppliers are in the favored position that the red hot curve of figure 1 applies to them. Usually the typical demand curve applies: the more you want to sell, the lower your bargaining power gets, and your profitability per unit decreases. All product-centered businesses dream of being in the position of the red hot curve. Imagine that demand was so extensive that with every piece sold, more people want your product. Your economy of scale increases because you are able to produce less expensively and your profitability soars. Is that really just a dream? In 1908 Hans Wilsdorf coins a brand name with which to sign his creations: "Rolex." The rest is just history of marketing and product "wow." Today Rolex is the third largest watch company in the world with over $1.9 billion in sales. They are focused and only have two collections with a total of twenty-two and fourteen basic models respectively. As having Rolex on the wrist has become a synonym for urbane wealth, many nouveau rich from emerging countries just want to wear one as soon as they can afford it. There are no sales or specials, and the asking price is always paid without question. Therefore, Rolex is a prime example of simultaneous economy of scale and luxury branding. The brand carries a lot of "wow" and is red hot indeed!

The momentum product curve is in between the red hot and the typical demand curve: a product like the Sony Play Station 2 was hot for a while, but at a certain point, attractiveness of the product decreased, and it became a commodity product. Most momentum products face that destiny. But if you are able to put enough additional "extras" into your product, it may well be possible that it jumps on to the red hot curve and stays there.

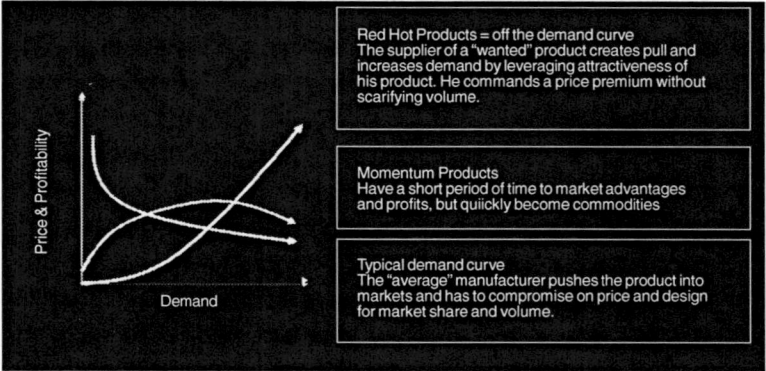

Figure 1: The Product Business

Other examples of current red hot products include the Pebble Beach Golf Club (or anywhere else you pay $250 for a round of golf or $2.50 per shot as an average golfer), the Palace Hotel in St. Moritz between Christmas and New Year (if you ask about the rates you, could not afford it anyway), and certain gimmicky cellular phones. In cell phones, the term "red hot" describes qualities/attributes that keep the phones competitive longer. Another example of "red hot" is, of course, tangible investments like real estate in hot areas of our nation (Southwest Florida, for instance).

Product "wows" can be created, and of course, product quality and product "wow" are related. Figure 2 shows these relationships and their interactions. According to Keki Bhote,[3] one of the creators of *The Ultimate Six Sigma*, there are twenty characteristics of a product or service that are of interest to customers.

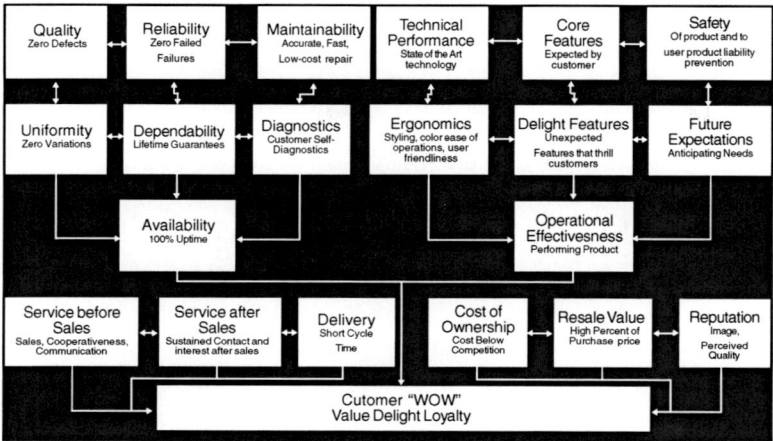

Figure 2: Network of Customer "Wow" for Products

The twenty characteristics are divided into four sections. First, a product has to be available. This refers to quality, uniformity, reliability, dependability, maintainability, and diagnostics. Secondly, the product has to be effective. This refers to technical performance, ergonomics, core features, delight features, safety, and anticipating future expectations of customers. Thirdly, the sales process, delivery, and the after-sales service have to be in line with or better than customer expectations. Fourthly, price, value, and reputation have to match

If you are in a service-centered business, the key is to create value for your customers while reducing the costs of providing these services, i.e., creating leverage for your delivery. The average service provider faces a challenge. The more value he wants to provide to his clients, the more time and effort he has to invest. This may be a true problem if you charge by the hour, considering that you only have approximately twelve hours a day you can bill. An attorney, for example, is generally limited in his/her billings to 1,800 to 2,000 hours per year. On the other hand, clients pay their professional service providers what they feel their hour is worth. It is very difficult to increase the hourly rates once you are in a certain bracket. If the results a service provider achieves are excellent, getting paid for the results is certainly a more-lucrative position than receiving an hourly rate. This is the reason why more and more clients and providers are looking for leverage and tend to agree to success-based contracts. This marked a correction in 2002 that hit the management consulting field hard but with good reason. During the golden decade, 1991 until 2002, the larger consulting firms got used to frequently implanting their consultants into the bodies of their host client companies like parasites into the veins of a warm-blooded mammal. These consultants often conducted work that could have been done very well by the client himself/herself. This is not what I mean by leverage in the service industry. As a provider of "red hot services," you want to be in the position where your added value to the client is such that he/she does not care what you bill—whatever the costs, it is worth it. James Champy calls this the "X" in his book *X-Engineering the Corporation*.[4] The story behind the "X" is that "in the early 1900s, GE was experiencing problems with one of the huge generators it manufactured at the company's plant in Schenectady, New York. When no one could figure out how to fix it, GE called in the great electrical engineer Charles Proteus Steinmetz, who duly spent several days examining the machine and all its drawings. After he departed, GE engineers found a large *X* chalked on the generator casing. A note from Steinmetz instructed them to cut the casing open at that spot and remove a certain number of turns of wire from the stator. The generator would then work—and so it did. Asked to name his fee, Steinmetz billed GE the at-that-time immense amount of $1,000. When GE's bean counters requested a detailed invoice justifying the charge, Steinmetz detailed his bill: (1) marking chalk *X* on the side of the generator: $1; (2) knowing where to mark chalk *X*: $999." This example clearly underscores the fact that once you are truly adding value (as the "X"-engineer did), you can fairly charge for it, and nobody considers these billings inappropriate.

TOTAL CUSTOMER FOCUS

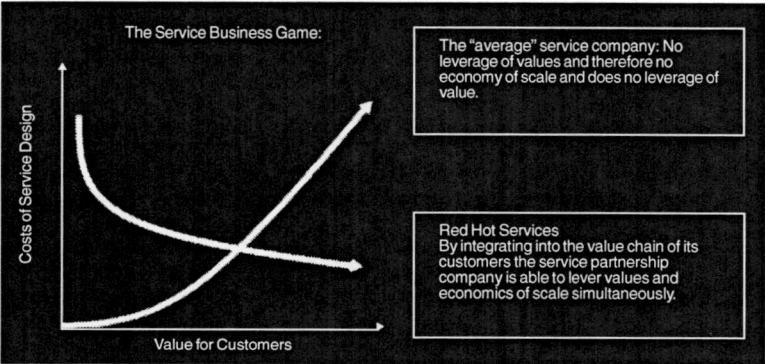

Figure 3: The Service Business

A good example of today's "red hot services" may be found at the Kinko's copy shop chain (which was recently acquired by FedEx). Kinko's is more than just a copy shop, it is a business network. Of course, you can get your copies made at Kinko's, as at any other copy shop. But the secret of the true value chain is far different than at any other copy shop chain in the world. You can post your documents on the Kinko's Web site, kinkos.com, and have them bound or even collated into presentations throughout the network. If you have a presentation, let's say, in Boston, Massachusetts, you can post your documents on the kinkos.com server wherever you are at the moment and have them printed, plotted, bound, and delivered to a certain address in Boston. Furthermore, Kinko's offers the customer services like video conferencing at its store locations, shopping for office supplies twenty-four hours a day, seven days a week and, of course, copying all kinds of documents. No wonder Kinko's claims that many Fortune 500 companies stopped investing in expensive equipment, but chose to completely outsource document management with Kinko's. The scalability of the network is what makes the service "red hot" for every type of customer.

The ultimate "wow" service again is the result of a network of elements. Communication, cooperativeness, dependability, timeliness quality, and operational effectiveness are the factors of a multiplication that equal a customer "wow" for services.[5] If one of these factors is zero, the result will be zero.

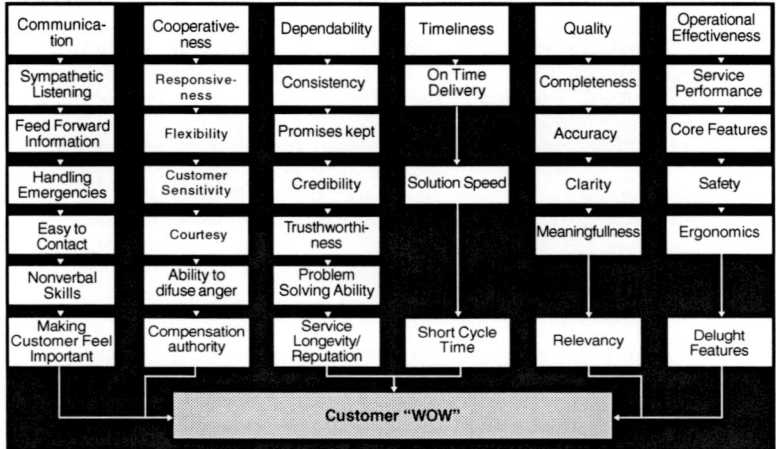

Figure 4: Network of Customer "Wow"

The quality of communication is the first measurement factor of a service. If the service provider listens sympathetically, feeds forward all information required, is able to handle emergencies, is easy to contact, and has excellent nonverbal skills, the customer feels important and heard. Cooperativeness, i.e., responsiveness, flexibility, customer sensitivity, courtesy, ability to diffuse anger, and compensation authority are the second measurement factor. If services are of consistent quality, promises are kept, the service provider is credible all the time, trustworthy, and able to solve any problems that occur, reputation will soar, and dependability is built up. Timeliness of delivery, solution speed, and short cycle time are next important. Only then traditional quality measurements like completeness, accuracy, clarity, meaningfulness, and relevancy come into play. Finally, effectiveness is measured in service performance, core features, safety, ergonomics, and delight features. All this leads to a customer "wow." Over Easter break this year, my son's car was hit in the side by a woman pulling backward out of her driveway in our home town Naples, Florida. She left her card and my son met her Easter Sunday to assess and discuss the damage. One hour later—on Easter Sunday—we got a call from the lady's insurance company to schedule my son's car for the body shop the following Tuesday. This was somewhat complicated because my son studies at the University of Miami and of course wanted to take his car with him. So the insurance company double-checked and called back a few minutes later just to tell us that they would not only take care of the repair, but also supply a rental car and a pager (to notify when the repair was done) for the duration the car was unavailable. Impeccable service, all "wow" elements met! This even let us forget the inconvenience of the incident.

Do customers really care if you, as their supplier, are in a specific type of industry? I do not think so. What truly matters for them is the kind of specific solution they get from their supplier, regardless of the value chain. Therefore, modern business definitions are not bound to any specific industry, but rather to a particular solution delivered or skills in a specific process. Most often, this solution is based on integrating into the customer's value chain over time. The business engineer blends into his customer's processes. Such relationships are frequently based on a considerable investment of time and out-of-pocket expense. Over time, however, the harvest can be continuous and long term.

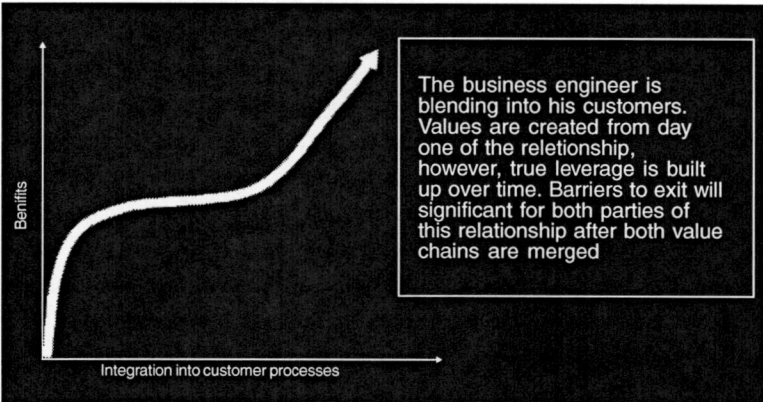

Figure 5: The Wow Business

Servisco[6] in Warsaw, Poland (today the company's name is DHL) was the vanguard of the Deutsche Post logistics network in Poland. The network included Danzas freight forwarding, EuroExpress parcel services, and DHL. Servisco salespeople did much more than try to sell parcel services to their customers; they went to their customers and offered them a complete analysis of their logistics processes. Based on the data generated, they proposed the best solution for all of the prospective customers' logistics problems. If it helped the customer, this even included adding competitors as service providers to the proposal. Their business model was based on their mission of being the favored goods mobility provider for Polish customers. This business definition allowed Servisco to claim a leading position, although they were not yet the largest logistics company in Poland. The business model Servisco found in 2002 was a cornerstone for the transformation of Deutsche Post World Net, Danzas, and DHL into DHL as we know it today. This is what business definition is all about: find a business definition that allows you to be special and different, and give yourself a chance to create the "wow."

GM's OnStar™[7] Network is another example of smart business engineering. Cars equipped with OnStar are much safer than cars without the service. In the event a front airbag deploys, the vehicle sends a signal to the OnStar center. An advisor will attempt to contact the driver, inquiring whether or not she needs assistance. If the driver can't answer, emergency help will be notified, and the location of the car will be provided. If you find yourself or another person in a situation where you need immediate assistance from police, fire, or emergency medical services (EMS), you can press the red emergency button. Your location information is transmitted to the OnStar Center and your call takes priority status on an advisor's screen. Even if the person who needs help does not have OnStar, you can alert an advisor. Within seconds, an OnStar advisor can contact the nearest emergency service provider with your location and your request for help. If you determine that your vehicle has been stolen, you can contact an OnStar advisor. OnStar will help the police determine its whereabouts. This is a home game for law enforcement because OnStar provides deputies with the vehicle location, and most police forces are equipped with compatible tracking devices. Just give the advisor your PIN and they'll send a signal to unlock your door (if available on your vehicle). You can even have it delayed up to fifteen minutes to give you enough time to get to your vehicle. Or, if you remembered that you forgot to lock your doors once you're away from your vehicle, an advisor can send a signal to lock them for you (if available on your vehicle). And there are many more features like driving directions, road side assistance, remote diagnostics, concierge services, just to name a few. GM really integrated itself into the mind of the drivers of its cars. Plans start at $16.95 per month and are worth a "wow" every penny.

And why is this "wow" so important? Tom Peters [8] said that providing memorable "experiences" is a big deal. "Experience" is quite a contrast to "product" or "service." Delivering a kick beats providing "good stuff." Leaving an indelible memory is better than a product that works. Customers that want more are really happy and overly glad they bought that experience. Really happy customers want to be member of your club and become word-of-mouth viral-marketing agents. They not only get what they pay for but are surprised and delighted at every turn. Without differentiation there would only be commodities. Differentiation guru Seth Godin[9] said that the problem with being remarkable is actually the problem with fear. If you (your products, your services, your company, your business model) are different, it is likely that some people will not like you and that is what most executives are afraid of. My point is that if you segmented correctly, a lot of people will love you and some may not love you. Those who love you will be fans cheering for you and asking for more differentiation. Eventually these loyal customers start referring you to their friends and contacts and your business will soar at nearly no marketing costs. EBay has the highest referral rate of customers (75 percent) and the lowest costs of all e-businesses to acquire a customer ($10). That is more than three times lower than Amazon ($34). Why? Because eBay is different. It is a $24 billion business. It even allows people to develop their own retail business on the backbone of the eBay network. Businesses like i-soldit.com are helped by eBay itself to develop a chain of drop-off stores. You drop off an item for sale, they photograph the item, write descriptive copy about it, and list it on eBay. They take care of payment, collection, packaging, and customer service. After your item sells, you just get a check. Customer quote that their services are awesome, and that they are addicted to them. Wow!

FOCUS ON ENTERPRISE VALUE ADDED

Do you always have to be a leader in size to be the most profitable in an industry? Not if you create enough differentiation to attract an adequate number of customers willing to pay for your specialty. An alert follower or specialist often has a valid business position. Typical industry leaders are like great white sharks that defend their territory. No other great white shark will be tolerated in this territory; immediate interception and defeat would be the reaction. The alert follower is rather comparable to a school of piranhas in a river in the Amazon. They know that they are not able to survive in the ocean where the great white shark is. Therefore, they look for their own specialty in a small spot of the river. They are aware that they cannot actively search for prey, but when an animal crosses the river, they will attack it as a group and get their prey with enormous and fierce speed. Both the market leader and the smaller business focusing on being first in their class have merit and substantial chances of survival. The problematic positions are those in the middle of the field. These organizations are either struggling with growth and shortages of cash or they do not create enough differentiation to achieve/earn premium price positions.

Michael Porter reflected the relationship of size and profitability most comprehensively in his masterpiece *Competitive Advantage: Creating and Sustaining Superior Performance*,[10] in which he set the standard for competitive positioning. Whereas the advantages of an agile, profitable company are obvious, the advantages of being a big player come with a challenge. Ted Turner's AOL was leading dial-up network connection as a global Internet Service Provider (ISP) in 2002 with thirty-five million members worldwide. However, they were not focusing on dominating the high-speed access field at that time. AOL only recognized this problem when they faced an exodus of subscribers. In the first quarter of 2003 alone, 176,000 U.S. subscribers changed to providers like Comcast or Verizon. Parallel Intel started to bet big on making wireless computing easier with their M4/Centrino processors supporting wireless fidelity (Wi-Fi), thus making dial-up unnecessary. Why should anyone pay for the use of AOL's dial-up software when they can just connect to the web through a TV-cable broadband or at a Wi-Fi hot spot anywhere on the globe? In a desperate attempt to regain its customer base, AOL started to bank on broadband and developed a software that could be used for dial-up and broadband simultaneously. In April 2003, they also began to focus more on delivering content from their parent company, Time Warner, via the AOL portal and their own AOL broadband platform. Advantages will be immense if AOL can retain most of its thirty-five million subscribers, even at a lower monthly rate than before, because through broadband they get a channel to deliver all the information and media content of Time Warner. Failure, however, would be catastrophic to AOL Time Warner, estimating that every subscriber lost equals at least $240 in potential annual revenue (thus the 176,000 accounts lost during the first quarter of 2003 sum up to a gap of $42 million per year). Size, therefore, always means leverage of both advantages and disadvantages. According to Porter, companies should try to achieve competitive advantage either by developing a strategy that would capitalize on its ability to match its competitors' offerings at lower costs, or by surpassing their offerings with a superior product or service at a higher price. For large companies this means focusing their innovation on ideas with a potentially large number of users and then applying economy of scale to serve these users at a lower cost than anybody else—including the user—could do it. Robert Metcalfe, founder of 3Com Corporation and designer of the Ethernet protocol, stated that the "usefulness, or utility, of a network equals the square of the number of its users." Metcalfe's law is best explained with the telephone. It is of very limited use if only you and your family have one. If a whole city is wired, usefulness increases significantly, but only if the whole world uses telephones, the utility of the system becomes phenomenal. The same applies for the internet. It reached critical mass early 1990 and today roughly 50 percent of the Western civilization is online. With large networks at their disposition, firms need to give their customers a reason why they should select them as their provider for a product or service. Either "wow" products (differentiation focus), or costs (scale focus). Consumers only buy from someone if buying is cheaper than the transaction costs involved if they conducted business with others using the market. Nobel laureate Ronald Coase explained the nature of transaction costs in 1937[11] stating that "firms and other economic organizations and institutions, in effect, exist because agents find it a useful manner of minimizing transactions costs." This also allows us to conclude that firms should conduct internally only those activities that cannot be performed more economically in the market or by another firm. The firm that masters this law best will become cost leader and therefore the market leader. It is either differentiation, cost leadership, or both that leads to enterprise value added.

How, then, do we add enterprise value in daily business life? Woody Allen once stated that "80 percent of success in life is just showing up." In the sixties and seventies, this philosophy/theory certainly applied to many businesses. Executives had learned that production capacity was the essential component to quickly rebuild the world after World War ll, and they applied this knowledge in managing their organizations. Willy Baumann, a good friend and entrepreneur, once told me the story of his father, who had owned and successfully led a shutter manufacturing company. This company had grown and flourished after the war, but like many other manufacturers, experienced some troubles in the crises of the late seventies, because it was just output oriented. In the late '90s Willy Jr. discussed the growth of his then company, Pendt (one of the leading Swiss store design and shop fitting companies with only major accounts in its portfolio), with his father Willy Sr.; the first advice offered was: "Willy, you have to increase output then the good numbers will follow." Apparently, times have changed!

When I entered the consulting business in the early '90s, the catch phrase of the day was "time to market." When we look at the success of large pharmaceutical companies at that time, the concept was certainly valid. If they had planned to enter the market after a five-year process of research and development, anticipating a twenty-year patent protection (fifteen basic and five extension), and if indeed they managed to enter the market earlier, this was pure cash in hand because the market was waiting for the products to come. In certain industries, this way of thinking still applies. Many of the e-commerce ventures of "e-crazy quartile 1998-2001" based their concepts on the hope that they would be able to develop profitable business ideas shortly after their market entry. This was only successful for the early movers like eBay and Amazon. Many others failed because most of them had no clue when they would be profitable, if ever. Profitability was no issue at all in the gold rush of the turn of the century. The stock market was sucking in every IPO promising the kick of a click. We all know what followed, and those believing that markets were perpetually bearish paid dearly. To make things worse, 9/11 happened, and the world changed forever in late 2001. If today you want to present any concept to a board of capitalists, you need to clearly state when your break-even point is going to be reached. However, the classical approach to reaching break-even implies that after this point manna is going to flow forever, and all you have to do is increase capacity to enhance profitability. Are we back in the seventies again? I do not think so, and I do not think that the concept mentioned above will allow companies to survive in the long term either. In 1998 Al Ehrbar from Stern Stewart wrote his book about Economic Value Added, EVA.[12] Amazingly enough, four years before the Enron and Worldcom cases he stated that U.S. GAAP and IAS were wrongheaded and set overly lax guidelines for accounting. Consequently, Stern Stewart had developed their own way of rating companies in terms of their real profitability. EVA is a cash-out / cash-in based entrepreneurial approach to return on total capital and hardly allows accounting tricks like deferred depreciation or discounted future profits. It also applies costs of opportunity to debt, i.e., requesting that debt earns its costs (interest), plus the expected entrepreneurial return on equity. The concept has the following key points.

- Until a business returns a profit that is greater than its cost of capital, it operates as a loss. EVA is a measure of true profits. It is after-tax operating profits minus the appropriate capital charge for both debt and equity. Interest paid on debt is not capital charge but cost. The capital charge is the hypothetical return on the capital markets for an investment of similar risk. As debt is always related to equity and the creditor could theoretically use his leverage for other businesses, debt has to return its interest to the lender plus the same capital charge as equity.
- EVA = NOPAT - C%(TC), where NOPAT is net operating profits after taxes, C% is the percentage cost of capital, and TC is total capital (total debt + total equity).
- MVA is exactly equal to the stock market's equivalent of the net present value, or NPV of a company. It is a company's market value minus the book value of its invested capital (adjusted accounting book value, because GAAP is wrongheaded).
- MVA = Market value—Total Capital

Peter Drucker[13] stated that "until a business returns a profit that is greater than its cost of capital, it operates at a loss. Never mind that it pays taxes as if it had a genuine profit. The enterprise still returns less to the economy than it devours in resources . . . Until then it does not create wealth; it destroys it." Put simply: When managers employ capital in projects, they have to pay for it just as if it were a wage. EVA is net operating profit minus an appropriate charge for the opportunity cost of all capital invested in an enterprise. As such, EVA is an estimate of true "economic" profit, or the amount by which earnings exceed or fall short of the required minimum rate of return that entrepreneurs, shareholders, and lenders could get by investing in other ventures or securities of comparable risk.

My bet is that this concept is going to become the measurement for success in the first decade of 2000. Currently common EVA rates are in the range of 8 to 12 percent. This straight focus on investor return should also influence how companies innovate. Should a company make one big bet on a significant investment or many smaller bets with lower capital employed? The Whirlpool Corporation decided to go the low risk / high reward avenue. Over 68,000 ideas have been created since 1999. Most ideas are only awarded small development budgets not higher than $20,000 and only the best ideas get to the market. Such hits included a clothes vitalizing system (Personal Valet™) that refreshes clothes in about thirty minutes with heat activated mist. It frees consumers from the ironing board. They also launched an in-sink dishwasher that cleans dishes three times faster than a full-size dishwasher, and the Gladiator™ garage works system offering a rugged, coordinated organization system for every man's sanctuary. There is no doubt that all these innovations are severe EVA creators, because the investments were relatively low and margins on the products generally are high. On the other hand, the Walt Disney Corporation typically plays it big to grow. A new resort is an investment of several hundred million dollars and does not necessarily work as planned from the beginning. The Disneyland Resort Paris missed targets for its first few years after opening in 1992, and it only got going after significant repositioning and even further investments. One problem was the assumption that the central location in Europe would be ideal. A glance at the map confirms that all roads of central Europe lead into Paris. Unfortunately, the climate in Europe is not like in California or Florida and even in the summertime it may rain for weeks. Also the Parisians did not wait for an American amusement park to be opened in their backyard. Big bets have the flip side of big risks, and it was an open secret that Euro-Disney was a loss operation for its first four years after opening in 1992. Between 1996 and 2003 Disney invested $9.8 billion in theme parks. Although the company depreciated $4.3 billion on that capital expenditure these depreciations are not relevant for EVA. Disney shareholders expect double-digit returns of their invested capital. In 2003 Disney had operating income of $957 million from park operations. This is about 10 percent or double digit but does not constitute an EVA of 10 percent, because operating income does not include interest expenses ($793 million consolidated for the group) and income taxes ($789 million consolidated for the group). It may be assumed that park operations of Disney have a very low EVA.

KNOW YOUR UNCERTAINTY

Find out where the masses are going and then run like hell to get four steps ahead of them.
—Tom Peters about Ghandi Leadership

By 1920 Gandhi[14] had developed his vision of India becoming a leading competitor in world economy. He did not dare to communicate this to the British colonialists, nor to his fellow Indians. He knew of the risks of either imprisonment or assassination. Starting in 1921, he began to accomplish his mission in small steps. Tom Peters reflects on this approach in *The Circle of Innovation*.[15] Peters reminds us that we still have to accomplish some results in our daily business to make our living, and while doing so we should try to achieve our repositioning for the future. Economic pressure, of course, is significant, because according to this concept the strategist is on his own in creating the resources for his strategy. To make things even more challenging, the communicative world allows us to do nearly everything today and may divert our focus. Most of you may not know the textile industry. However, let us assume you decide to become a shirt manufacturer one day. Without any problems, you could find a manufacturer of cotton fabric in China over the Web. It would also be no challenge to identify a sewing sweatshop for shirts in Bangladesh or Pakistan on the Internet. Designs and patterns are available from many designers in Europe at little cost. Correctly, you would focus solely on your Unique Selling Proposition (USP) for your shirts. You would be on the lookout for Global Positioning System (GPS) chips from Silicon Valley and you would want to implant them into your shirts. Your pitch would be to manufacture an executive shirt or blouse where every spouse would know exactly where her husband is at any given moment. Is this a dream? No, you could actually easily realize this innovation almost instantly. The problem is that we can do almost everything at any time even with little capital. Business administration calls this the "fish tank phenomenon": You never know what young whiz kids are doing out there at this moment. Maybe they are directing a webcam at their fish tank (aquarium), linking it to a Web site, and attracting hundreds of thousands of hits with viral marketing based on referrals from user to user. A modern "fish tank" is Google. Google's founders Larry Page and Sergey Brin developed a new approach to online search that took root in a Stanford University dorm room in September 1998 and quickly spread to information seekers around the globe. Since then the company has expanded to more than 1,900 employees and is now widely recognized as the world's largest search engine—an easy-to-use free service that usually returns relevant results in a fraction of a second.[16] "Googol" is the mathematical term for a 1 followed by one hundred zeros. The term was coined by Milton Sirotta. Google's play on the term reflects the company's mission to organize the immense amount of information available on the Web.

These unlimited opportunities force us to focus. The risk in focusing is best expressed by Albert Einstein, who stated that "things must be made as simple as possible, but not simpler." Vilfredo Pareto was the first scientist to publish the 80/20 principle in 1897. Richard Koch explains the application of the law brilliantly in his book *The 80/20 Principle: The Secret of Achieving More With Less.*[17] In 1949 Harvard professor of philology George K. Zipf rediscovered and elaborated

Pareto's law and it became famous as "Zipf's Principle of Least Effort." Zipf based his law on the experience that 20 to 30 percent of any resource accounted for 70 to 80 percent of the activity related to that resource. IBM was one of the early users of Zipf's law in management. In 1963, they found out that 20 percent of the operating code was using 80 percent of a computer's operating resources. After reassessing resources to the most used 20 percent of a computer and rewriting operating system codes, IBM was able to make their computers faster than most of their competitors. Colin Powell refers to Zipf's law in executive decision making in lesson no. 15 of his *A Leadership Primer*.[18] He states in part 1: "Use the formula P=40 to 70, in which *P* stands for the probability of success and the numbers indicate the percentage of information acquired." Part 2: "Once the information is in the 40 to 70 range, go with your gut." An executive has to learn how to deal with uncertainty in his or her specific way. Timely decisions most often only account for 15 percent or even less of all efforts, but they have a significant impact on success. Every organization has to focus its resources on realization. Once the direction is "true north" and the organization goes full steam ahead with clear decisions, these efforts only account for less than 15 to 20 percent of success.

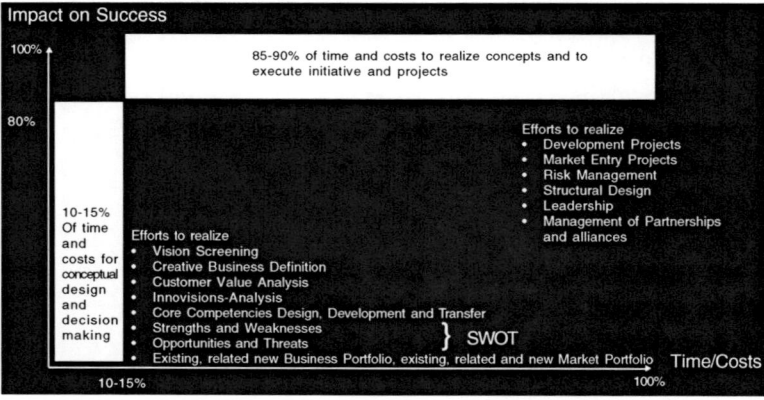

Figure 6: Pareto in Management

The bottom line of this concept is the not-too-bold idea of thinking before doing. The following are some ideas on how to apply Pareto's and Zipf's findings in practice.

In his book *Straight from the Gut*[19] Jack Welch made a point about how he assesses existing business with a five-question "acid" test:

- "What is the detailed global position of your business and that of your competitors: market shares, strengths by product line and by region today?
- What actions have your competitors taken in the past two years that have changed the competitive landscape?
- What have you done in the last two years to alter that landscape?
- What are you most afraid your competitors might do in the next two years to change the landscape?
- What are you going to do in the next two years to leapfrog any of their moves?"

GE is a pragmatic and straightforward money machine. Therefore, any executive who is able to answer these questions must have done his/her homework, i.e., have a strategy and be able to contribute to GE's goals. Bottom line: In order to respond adequately you must have a clear picture and a goal.

Hugh Courtney[20] comes up with new insight about the concept of incorporating levels of uncertainty into strategic development. He calls the concept "20/20 Foresight" referring to the American standard of clear vision (in Europe this would be the equivalent of zero diopters, i.e., clear vision on both eyes). Strategy development has become very challenging in our volatile times, and he reflects on these difficulties in what he calls four levels of uncertainty.

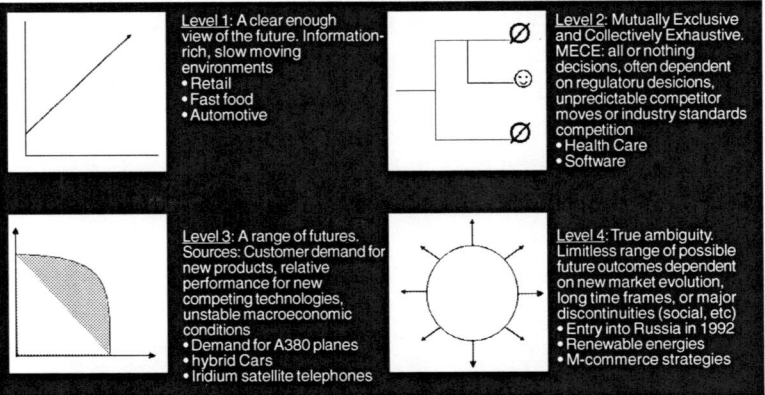

Figure 7: Levels of Uncertainty

If you have a sufficiently clear view of the future and your environment is information rich and slow moving, you can often read your strategic options like a putting line on a green in golf: There is only one way to get the ball into the hole. This is a level 1 uncertainty, i.e., you have a clear picture of the present and the future. Level 1 applies to demographically driven industries like grocery stores, hospitality, and fast food. An example of a level 1 shaping story is ALDI. When ALDI opened its first store in Essen, Germany, in 1948, they rocked the German grocery industry with a limited assortment concept of six hundred articles at rock bottom prices. The traditional grocery industry was clearly at level 1 and wanted everybody in its club to adapt and coast on the stream of easy growing business. All of a sudden, a shaper had entered the market and pursued the 80/20 principle in grocery. Instead of the usual twenty-five thousand items a traditional grocery store carries, they focused on the six hundred most needed and most used products in the average home. Their Web site states "ALDI is a limited assortment discount international retailer, specializing in an assortment of private label, high quality products at the lowest possible prices. Our unique way of operating makes it virtually impossible for competitors to match our combination of price and quality. This means value to our customers and after all, value is buying quality products at low prices."[21] ALDI shaped a level 1 industry. Today ALDI is the world leading grocery chain operating more than five thousand stores worldwide and over seven hundred stores in twenty-six states of the United States. Shapers need a lot of spine in a level 1 environment. They will not be welcome

In level 2 uncertainties, you most often have options that are mutually exclusive and collectively exhaustive. If you are dependent on regulators, for example, and a new law passes, it may be very clear what you have to do and what you cannot do. In golf, this is like having the option to go over the water with your second shot, or to lie up near the green and use three shots to get there. If you hit your second one well and make the green in regulation, you will putt for a birdie—if the ball gets wet, you cannot reach the green with less than four shots (you already took two, plus one penalty and the next shot). If you play it safe and lie up, the best you can score at this hole will be a par. Consequently, you have to make up your mind: Do you prefer a chance for a birdie, or do you want a safe par? In business, such uncertainties apply to utilities, the pharmaceutical industry, and the software industry. A typical level 2 example is Apple versus Microsoft. McIntosh lost the standard operating system battle against Windows, and although Apple was the pioneer and lead technology, Microsoft managed to tailgate so fast that they could take over the initiative and outpace McIntosh in the quest of becoming the standard in the industry. The lesson learned from this example is to watch the rearview mirror constantly. Competitors in the mirror may be closer than they appear. When smart and strong shapers see an opportunity to bypass potential standard-setters they will, and they take it all. Pfizer developed Viagra, a drug to treat erectile difficulties. It was a revolutionary treatment against erectile dysfunction (ED) when launched in 1998. Viagra was launched the classical way and introduced to medical doctors who were supposed to sell the product to their patients. The problem was that potential patients did not know about the drug and usually pysicians did not ask their patients during an exam "and by the way, can I also help you with your ED?" Demand initially was slow for the drug until Pfizer launched a concentrated marketing campaign to educate the male target group. All of a sudden patients would ask their doctors about Viagra, and the drug started to take off. This was the right moment for Lilly ICOS to launch Cialis, which works twice as fast as Viagra and lasts up to thirty-two hours longer. Practically at the same time Bayer and Glaxo Smith Kline launched Levitra. Pfizer had done the pathfinder work and had shaped the market on the assumption that they would be able to harvest on the $1.6 billion market primarily themselves. The two other contenders were smart adapters and just waited until the markets were ready for their products and followed with speed to market. Level 2 environments can be very rewarding if the outcomes are under control (Microsoft versus Apple). Level 2 can be very frustrating if contenders of equal strength start to fight for the lead over the next switch.

If the range of possible outcomes is very wide but still foreseeable, you are at level 3 of uncertainty. In golf, this would be me on the tee of a long par five and playing for money. My drive could very well be 220 yards straight down the fairway. On the other hand, it could land anywhere in an angle of 180 degrees, and I would not know why. Alternatively, if I played a five iron I could be even better off on this difficult hole. What should I do? In the airplane industry of 2003, Airbus was relying on an integrated family of planes from A318, with a capacity of 100, to A380, with a capacity of 555 passengers. However, Airbus mainly focused on commercial aircrafts. Boeing, on the other hand, was much broader in its offerings of defense systems, air traffic management, and commercial airplanes. Each commercial airplane model was actually a system in itself: 717, 737 next generation, 747-400, 757, 767, and 7E7. The more-segmented approach is underlined with specialties like the commercial freighter BC-17X with powered cargo lifts and short field accessibility. In level 3 environments, the key is to have the information that lets you focus on the right angle of the potential range of probabilities. All competitors must have a certain size and enough resources to pursue their strategy of pushing the industry to what they consider the right angle. At level 3, the big league plays in its own conferences. Sometimes niches open up. After it was clear that neither Airbus nor Boeing would cater the thirty—to eighty-seat market, Embraer and Bombardier successfully entered the vacuum with offerings of regional jets in that specific segment. Whereas this fight is still ongoing, the telecom industry experienced a shift from level 3 to level 2 after the battle between Motorola's Iridium satellite telephone system and global system for mobile communication (GSM) was won by the GSM protocol. GSM now fights against the universal mobile telecommunication system (UMTS) in a level 2 environment. UMTS licenses were auctioned off by the regulators at extreme premiums ($60 billion in Germany alone). If marketed to consumers at a price to amortize those premiums, UMTS will have to perform a lot better than GSM to convince over 850 million users in 195 countries to change the systems to which they subscribe. Multiband terminals and the common use of wireless fidelity (Wi-Fi) protocols for broadband wireless internet access, however, will most probably push GSM off the track. For telecommunication providers this pattern implies that they have to invest heavily in old and new technologies just to get a chance to stay in the market.

If there is true ambiguity about the potential outcomes, you are in a level 4 situation. This would be the equivalent of playing in a golf tournament where the format is team skins for money, but you do not know your teammates because the hosts are raffling the players. There is a nearly unlimited number of outcomes; just by signing up, you could get into a hammer group and earn a lot of money, on the other hand, you could be teamed up with rookies and lose a ton. Every larger organization had to consider being present in Russia when the curtain fell in 1992. Nobody knew what would happen, but presence was important in order to occupy key territory in early stages. The switch from level 4 to level 3 or 2 may happen fast. When Courtney wrote his book in 2001, he stated that M-commerce strategies (mobile telephone commerce) would be level 4. In May 2003, I conducted a marketing training course with Encorus[22] (a company that belongs to eONE Global, which furthermore is held by First Data, which also owns Western Union). They had just developed a virtual wallet software standard to shoot M-commerce into a level 2 environment. Encorus developed the mobile wallet software that allows telecommunication providers to become payment administrators for value added services. The solutions are simple but ingenious: Throughout Estonia you buy your parking tickets by short message service, SMS, and the fees are charged to your mobile phone bill. In Berlin, Germany, the local transport authority allows you to buy tickets by SMS. After dialing an SMS number when entering a bus, subway, tram or train the ticket is delivered instantly to the mobile phone as a message and billed to the phone account. Encorus also makes sure the service is secure and reliable. Currently Encorus is the world market leader in mobile wallet technology and owns the level 2 tracks it is on.

Depending on your level of uncertainty, your strategic options in shaping the industry or adapting to the industry are different. As shown in the next figure, in level 1 it is better to adapt, whereas levels 2 and 3 offer opportunities for both successful shaper and adapter strategies. Level 4 clearly favors the shaper, because he can bring the industry from a level 4 to a level 3 situation, or even 2 if he takes the initiative and starts shaping the industry.

	Level 1	Level 2	Level 3	Level 4
S h a p e	• Create an industry standard • Introducing product, service, or business system innovations • Restructuring the industry • Replicating existing business systems in new markets • Influencing competitor's conduct	• Create strategies are designed to create industry upheaval • Seek to create chaos out of order • Risky and uncommon	• Create order out of chaos • When a limited set of possible outcomes—in which one of them will occur—can be identified, shaping strategies focus on making the right one occur	• Shaping Strategies focus on moving the industry toward the "right end of the range" • Direction-setting strategies	• The Shaper can bring the market to order • The more uncertain the environment, the greater the chances that a anyone willing to take a standmay be emulated by others
A d a p t	• Following a potential shaper's lead • Hedging against future possible outcomes • Probing through continuous experimentation • Building a flexible organization	• Adapting is the traditional choice • Strategies build around superior execution advantages	• Hallmark is the flexibility to compete and potentially thrive—regardless of which one of the distinct industry outcome occurs • Adapters must only prepare for a limited set of possible outcomes	• Focus on more emergent strategy development • Successful adapter strategies are supplemented with an increasing focus on monitoring market developments over	• Focus on strategy as organization—making sure to have the right people, systems, culture and governance processes in place to identify and adapt to opportunities as they become clarified over time

Figure 8: Shape or Adapt?

TAKE YOUR SHOT

The key in business development is to come up with a structured approach to identifying new challenges. The following flowchart explains the very basic but challenging approach of identifying the most promising options out of either generic or accidental developments.[23] Traditionally, companies innovate based on their competencies and resources. This is called an "inside-in" approach, where "inside" represents the current competencies and resources and "in" is the business development process. Many revolutionary innovations would never have been implemented if it were not for this approach. Some geniuses in R&D come up with ideas never heard of before and bless us with milestone developments like the laptop PC or the digital camera. If they asked the customer of his opinions about their ideas, they would not get anywhere because their ideas are too revolutionary for the customer to appreciate. The fax machine on the other hand is an example how long time to market of an inside-in innovation can take. The use of the fax machine to transmit images via telephone lines did not become common in businesses until the late 1980s, but the technology dates back to the nineteenth century. The patent to the fax machine was granted May 27, 1843, in England, thirty-three years before the telephone. Alexander Bain (1818-1903) devised an apparatus comprised of two pens connected to two pendulums, which in turn were joined to a wire that was able to reproduce writing on an electrically conductive surface. In 1862, the Italian physicist Giovanni Caselli built a machine he called a "pantelegraph" (implying a hybrid of pantograph and telegraph), which was based on Bain's invention but also included a synchronizing apparatus. His pantelegraph was used by the French Post and Telegraph agency between Paris and Marseilles from 1856 to 1870. Elisha Gray (1835-1901), an American inventor, born in Barnesville, Ohio, invented and patented many electrical devices, including a facsimile transmission system. He also organized a company that later became the Western Electric Company. In 1902, Arthur Korn (1870-1945) of Germany invented telephotography, a means for manually breaking down and transmitting still photographs by means of electrical wires. In 1907, Korn sent the first intercity fax when he transmitted a photograph from Munich to Berlin. In 1925, Edouard Belin (1876-1963) of France constructed the Belinograph. His invention involved placing an image on a cylinder and scanning it with a powerful light beam that had a photoelectric cell which could convert light, or the absence of light, into transmittable electrical impulses. The Belinograph process used the basic principle upon which all subsequent facsimile transmission machines would be based. In 1934, the Associated Press introduced the first system for routinely transmitting "wire photos," and thirty years later, in 1964, the Xerox Corporation introduced Long Distance Xerography (LDX). For many years, facsimile machines remained cumbersome, expensive, and difficult to operate, but in 1966 Xerox introduced the Magnafax Telecopier, a smaller, forty-six-pound (17 kg) facsimile machine that was easier to use and could be connected to any telephone line. Using this machine, a letter-sized document took about six minutes to transmit. The process was slow, but it represented a major technological step. In the late 1970s, Japanese companies entered the market, and soon a new generation of faster, smaller, and more-efficient fax machines became available.[24]

TOTAL CUSTOMER FOCUS 41

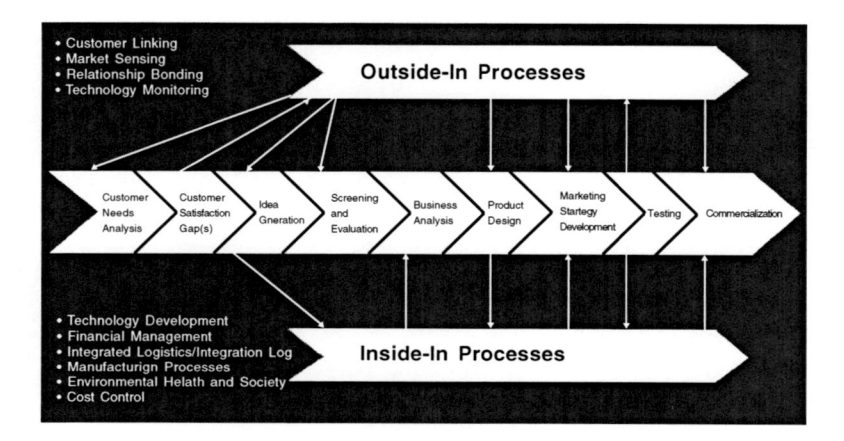

Outside-In Processes
- Customer Linking
- Market Sensing
- Relationship Bonding
- Technology Monitoring

Customer Needs Analysis → Customer Satisfaction Gap(s) → Idea Gneration → Screening and Evaluation → Business Analysis → Product Design → Marketing Startegy Development → Testing → Commercialization

Inside-In Processes
- Technology Development
- Financial Management
- Integrated Logistics/Integration Log
- Manufacturign Processes
- Environmental Helath and Society
- Cost Control

Figure 9: New Business Development

Endless time to market can be prevented by taking an outside-in approach beginning from the environment/market side. This outside-in view allows you to identify exposure to broad trends that need to pass through another filter to get to the relevant trends. A second filter evaluates the significance of all relevant trends. A third filter focuses on those trends having an impact on products and markets. In most cases, it is now possible to forecast the momentum of strategic business fields (products in markets) with or without those relevant trends. Trends themselves have certain potential directions in the future and need a forecast as well; and of course, it has to be determined what new opportunities and threats arise out of these trends. Consequently, all of these elements have a certain impact on the current and future strategy of an organization. The next step is to mirror opportunities and threats with customer perceptions to fill the gaps that need to be satisfied from the user's point of view. Pure inside-in development of products breeds incest. If organizations link an outside-in (i.e., the customer view) perspective with internal capabilities and potential, the results of business development are best. This concept is not at all new in business administration. However, why do companies neglect these rules so many times? A small medical device distributor invented a device called the Needle Destroyer.[25] This device is a perfect destroyer of hypodermic needles. Needlesticks are the most commonly occurring accident among healthcare professionals. Company founder Walter W. developed and launched the apparatus in 1998 to save nurses from needlesticks for good. So far this is a perfect idea to solve a long-existing problem. The company, however, forgot to have a really close look at the process of administering substances with needles. If this process is analyzed properly, there is no need for this device at all because in every hospital room there is a little box called the "sharps container." If the nurse takes this container to the cart she uses when providing her services to the patients and then drops the used needle into an attached plastic container, the process is as safe as it can be. The nurse can discard any sharp tool in the sharps container, not only needles. Apparently, the development of the Needle Destroyer was mainly an "inside-in" approach. The company failed to ask users about their real needs and demands while developing the product and as a result, the introduction of the Needle Destroyer was a multimillion dollar blunder.

A positive example of outside-in development is the Cargo Domino product of the Swiss Federal Freight Railway systems.[26] Cargo Domino is an integrated freight system based on exchangeable containers. These small (22.5 ft / 7450mm) containers can be transferred at any train station from the railway car to a light truck without the need of a crane or terminal equipment. The containers then reach their final destination where the truck may unload and leave the container for further use. The containers come in many variations like air-conditioned frozen food storage, sliding doors, canvas cover, etc., and have built-in stilts for storage off truck or railway car. The system was designed in cooperation with major grocery chains, truck operators, and freight railway specialists to cater the needs of smaller grocery chains and to combine the advantages of both rail and road.

Corporate systems are not just about innovation and business development. They are incredibly complex, and all of their elements influence strategies. In 1974, initiated by the first of the most recent economic downturns, Ulrich[27] tried bring light into organizational functioning with the four management layers of the St. Gallen

Management Model: normative management, management of the future competitive position, management of the current competitive position, and operative management. In 1980 Porter[28] introduced his three generic strategies and one of the most powerful competitive tools yet developed to bring structure to the task of strategic positioning: lowest cost, differentiation, and focus. After Bleicher[29] translated the St. Gallen approach into a guideline of how to manage companies, it became the management theory favored by most European management scholars. It combines all external and internal factors an organization faces into a single complex management system on four layers. The normative layer is the one that can be influenced least in the short term. The operative layer, of course, is the one that is tight at hand and can be influenced in the short term. Marketing management handles portfolios of the current competitive position while the future competitive position is handled by strategic management. For strategy development, it is important to remember that all elements of such a management system have to be considered when crafting a strategy. The following figure is a checklist I frequently used in strategy projects. I took a lot of complexity out of the even more-detailed St. Gallen charts about the management system and tried to make it a little bit more user friendly.

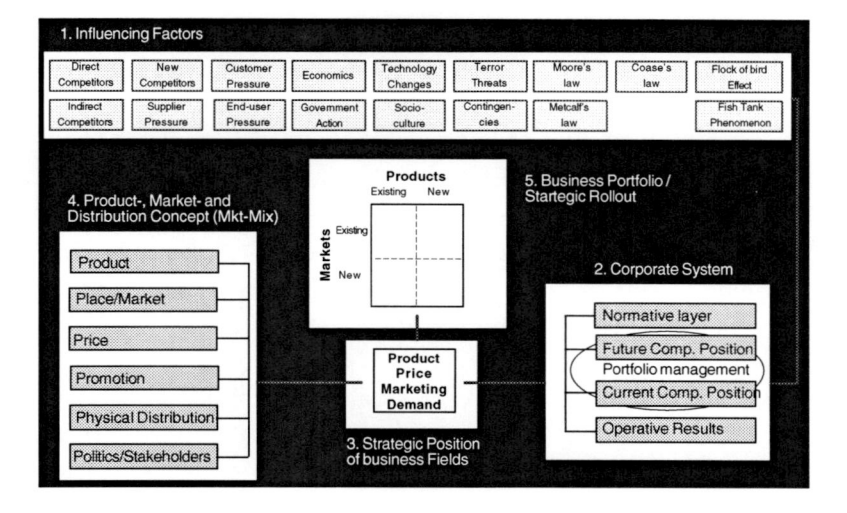

Figure 10: The Management System

My work as a strategy consultant and entrepreneur inspired me to come up with a slightly adapted concept of the St. Gallen Management Model as designed in figure 10. (1) I believe that before crafting a strategy you need to look at numerous forces that could potentially influence a business. Direct competitors and indirect competitors are the most obvious ones. More and more industries are threatened by indirect competitors—mostly attracted through changes in technology: Virgin Mobile[30] became a major player in prepaid cell phones within just one year. Their business concept is a simple prepaid plan and bears no contractual obligation to the user. Investments were low because Virgin piggybacks on Sprint's PCS network. Their pitch is to sell the Virgin experience with downloadable ring tones and Virgin music. Suppliers, users, and end users more and more become a major force in business. The overall economical outlook and government regulating action drive industries more than ever before and must be considered in the analysis. Sociocultural changes and technological development are obvious drivers of business opportunities. Since September 11, 2001, terrorist threats and contingencies (all things that can in no way be influenced by an average organization) have to be considered a major force for strategies.

There are five new forces I'm primarily looking at: First the pace of technological changes according to the law of Intel cofounder and chairman Emeritus Gordon Moore. Moore is widely known for Moore's law, in which he predicted that the number of transistors the industry would be able to place on a computer chip would double every couple of years. In 1995, he updated his prediction to once every two years. While originally intended as a rule of thumb in 1965, it has become the guiding principle for the industry to deliver ever-more-powerful semiconductor chips at proportionate decreases in cost.

The second new force I look at is Metcalfe's law which states that the usefulness or utility of a network equals the square of the number of its users. Robert Metcalfe, founder of 3Com Corporation and the designer of the Ethernet protocol for computer networks, observed that new technologies are valuable only if many people use them. The larger the population that uses your software, your network, your standard, your game, or your book, the more valuable it becomes, and the more new users it will attract, increasing both its utility and the speed of its adoption by still more users. There is a magical point of inflection at which a technology reaches critical mass. After that point its value increases exponentially.

The third new force is Ronald Coase's explanation of transaction costs, which measures the commercial sustainability of an idea. Coase concluded that firms are created because the additional cost of organizing them is cheaper than the transaction costs involved when individuals conduct business with each other using the market. Firms should only conduct those activities internally that cannot be performed more cheaply in the market or by another firm. Thus a firm will expand precisely to the point where "the costs of organizing an extra transaction within the firm becomes equal to the costs of carrying out the same transaction by means of an exchange on the open market."

The fourth new force is the "flock of bird" phenomenon by Craig Reynolds[31] which states that in many industries there is no clear leader and there seems to be chaos. Despite the fact that a market may look chaotic, the chaos theory states that there are still certain rules that can be simulated in artificial life. In the mid 80s Craig Reynolds applied the principles of artificial life to the phenomenon of birds flying in coordinated flocks. The challenge was to uncover simple rules that each bird (or boid) could follow that would produce flocking as an emergent behavior. Flocking is not a quality of any individual bird; it only emerges as a property of a group of birds. Each bird acts as an independent agent and obeys the simple rules. Reynolds identified three simple rules for each boid to follow within some given global parameters, and the result was an uncanny facsimile of flocking behavior unfolding itself on his computer screen. The general assumptions of the model are (1) each boid has an ability to sense local flockmates (sensory apparatus), (2) each boid can sense the whole environment (3D space), (3) all boids recalculate their current state (velocity vector) simultaneously once each time unit during the simulation. According to Reynolds, the rules of flocking behavior are (1) separation: steer to avoid crowding local flockmates; (2) alignment: steer toward the average heading of local flockmates; (3) cohesion: steer to move toward the average position of local flockmates. By looking at this phenomenon we try to find the hidden rules of industries that seem to be chaotic.

The fifth new force is what we call the fish tank phenomenon. Every kid can direct his webcam to his aquarium, launch this picture on a Web site, market the Web site as the greatest of them all, and create a new business. You do not know at which corner your next competitor is waiting and incumbency does not count anymore. In 1998 three college graduates of Florida Gulf Coast University founded a company known today as findwhat.com. In 2000 they went public and are listed at NASDAQ under FWHT. The findwhat.com network is an online marketplace that connects businesses with entities that are likely to purchase specific goods and services from the businesses' Web sites and provides an additional revenue stream to browser applications and Web sites which provide web directories, search engines or contextually relevant listings. They are the Yellow Pages of the Web and will replace the printed commercial listings soon. Today findwhat.com is already a money machine. In 2003 the company had revenues of $72 million and a net income after tax of $11.7 million. By the end of 2003 the company had $74 million in assets and only $10 million in current liability.

All the factors mentioned above influence the corporate system (2) which is the equivalent of the St. Gallen model. Imagine Atlas carrying your globes—your portfolio bubbles—in his hands over his head. Atlas only eats candy bars and your net operative results are one hundred candy bars per quarter. Out of those one hundred candy bars you draw what it takes to feed Atlas so he may be able to carry the globes well balanced over his head—this represents your current market position. If Atlas were forced to change the position of a globe, he would probably have to stretch out his arms. Have you ever tried to hold a ball away from your body with stretched arms? You will need much more energy for this position than for simply holding the ball over your head. Thus, to achieve a future competitive position (stretching the arms), Atlas will need many more candy bars than he did before to maintain his position. Either you have produced sufficient candy bars from your operative results, or you will need to ask the normative layer, i.e., the shareholders, to allow you to draw from the assets, or even worse, get candy bars on credit. The net of all candy bars you can manage to get will determine what competitive position you will finally be able to address. Each globe is held by four arms or factors influencing the position of a business field (3): product, price, marketing power, and demand. The price point and its equivalent costs significantly influence the size of your accessible market. Benefits provided by the product or service define its scalability. The more marketing power you are able to invest, the more you can promote benefits, as well as influence price and demand. The stability or volatility of demand defines the complexity of positioning a product in its markets. Each globe, or portfolio bubble, is divided into six continents or elements of the marketing mix (4). The continents are product, place, price, promotion, physical distribution, and politics/stakeholders. These elements of the marketing mix make the globe worth living on. Globes, however, do not stay at the same place all the time. Every globe has a different way to develop. This development is monitored in the strategic rollout (5). A product staying in the same market does not have the same requirements as a product evolving into new markets or markets that require the production of specific products. If a business field evolves itself out of scope it may well become a new product in a new market and thus may have very low chances for survival.

Complexity in business has increased logarithmically over the last few years. What used to be given relationships between manufacturer and vendors (B2V), trade (B2B), and users (B2C) is now a completely open environment. Could you have imagined researching the dealer invoice price of your car over the Web in 1990? Today, this is the first thing you do when you plan to buy a new vehicle. It goes as far as private consumers putting out requests for proposals when they are in the process of buying a car. GM and Ford both have Web sites allowing you to quickly search for cars and even to have financing offered in a click. As soon as you have decided what kind of deal you are interested in, they link you with a dealer. This situation was the other way around even a couple of years ago when consumers were totally dependent on car dealerships. Today, there is no more perishable thing than being incumbent. Today? Change has always been part of business life. Those who adapted or shaped survived, while those who slept hardly made it. Also, there seem to be windows of opportunity that open only for a certain length of time. Imagine if Greyhound had taken the opportunity to acquire an airline in the mid-1970s and had started introducing seamless mobility, combining land and air. Everybody would have recognized the greyhound on the company logo of a plane and marketing could most probably have been reduced to public relations. Every American would have accepted Greyhound's capability of being able to transport people from urban area A to urban area B, even internationally. Well, Greyhound did not see this window of opportunity open (they tried to open it at a later time) and instead of shaping America, their buses are still driving on the right lanes of the interstates, transporting those who cannot afford even rock-bottom airfares.

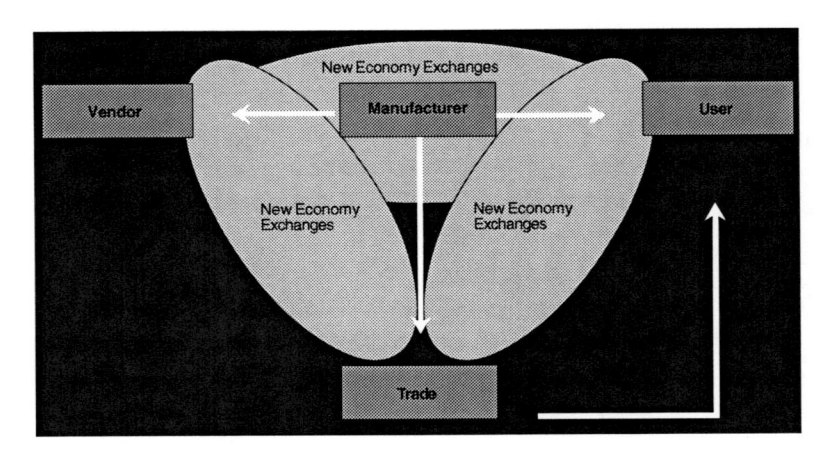

Figure 11: Incumbent Relationships Versus Dynamic Change

In areas where traditions dominate, such as Germany, France, and Japan, incumbent relationships can dramatically reduce a nation's competitiveness. In October 2002, *Wall Street Journal Europe*[32] published a report about the flittering competitiveness regarding productivity of Germany and France versus America. Both Germany and France have traditional trade systems consisting of trade associations and industry councils that only slowly adapt to new situations because the management of these institutions is highly political. In America this kind of institution never existed, and therefore the environment for change is much more dynamic, but also protected. If a European wants to order goods from an American e-commerce company such as Amazon, or eBay, complications arise. Most e-commerce companies do not ship overseas to people who don't have an American-funded credit card or a zip code from the United States.

The ability of being adaptive and flexible has been credited to small companies for a long time. Jack Welch[33] noted that this was a situation that the big players recognized relatively late. His findings were very logical because a dotcom company such as Amazon builds up its business gradually and therefore starts with expenses. Expenses are negative revenue. If you forget accounting and the flaws of USGAAP and its allowances of depreciation, these expenses are accumulating negative cash outs that are piling up. Once their gross margins (revenues minus costs of goods sold) are positive, dotcoms start amortizing their pile of cash outs. In spring 2002 Amazon announced their first positive quarter, i.e., the first time they were able to apply contribution margin to pay off the cash out. This is not so with big companies. They invest heavily into a venture and, of course, have a jump in cash out, i.e., an immediate expense exposure. Their resources, however, are tremendous and they can therefore accomplish projects with great speed. Shared resources throughout the divisions allow large organizations like GE to build up competencies with brute force. The payoff comes when the combined marketing and sales powers are utilized in a blitz launch of the concept based on existing resources that are adapted as needed. Therefore, the amortization time for innovations of big players is much shorter than for startups. Also, big players have the opportunity to buy any biz incubator at their leisure if they decide not to develop concepts themselves. Big is good once again.

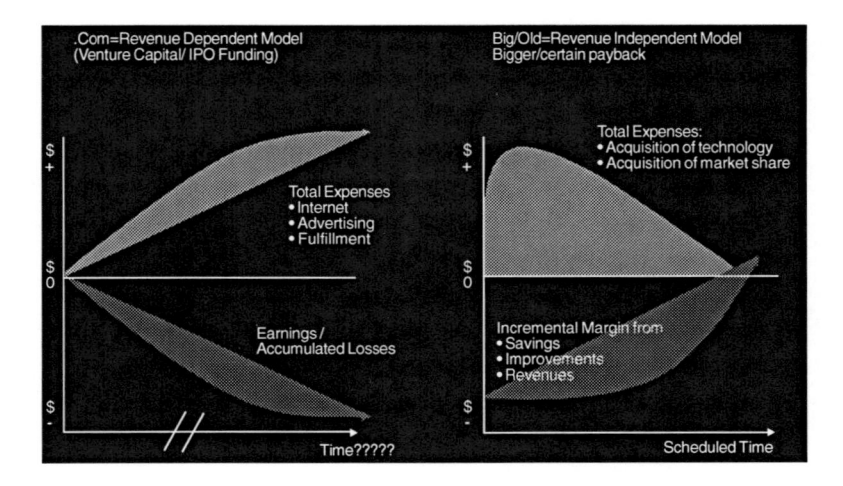

Figure 12: Big = Power

When Deutsche Telekom AG's T-Mobile USA entered the U.S. market they did it in the powerful way. Their first step was to acquire GSM provider VoiceStream in California to learn to understand the American market. T-Mobile is said to have paid over $5,000 per account in this acquisition. In a bold move, T-Mobile set up a GSM network with towers and antennas throughout the nation. Competitors like Sprint, Nextel, and Verizon did not consider a GSM network a threat to their PCS-based capabilities and let T-Mobile go on. It took about a year to establish broad nationwide coverage in GSM, and when the competitors started to realize what was happening it was too late. T-Mobile launched their nationwide GSM services in 2002 with an immense media campaign and immediately started to attract consumers. AT&T and Cingular were smart enough to cooperate with T-Mobile in distribution and network agreements and could stay abreast of T-Mobile with subscribers. Within less than two years, T-Mobile became provider number five in the United States with thirteen million subscribers, larger than Nextel and already 80 percent the size of Sprint (sixteen million subscribers).

There are three ways to take an idea or a product to market: integration, orchestration, or licensure. The integrator manages all steps to generate profits from an idea. The integrator may face steep investments to set up manufacturing facilities and to open distribution channels. Capability requirements for an integrator include strong cross-functional links within the organization, product design, and manufacturing process design skills, as well as the ability to source technical personnel. Integration of an idea is best used when speed to market is uncritical, the technology is proven, customer tastes are stable, and innovation is incremental.

If you do not want to integrate, orchestrating the idea may be a less-challenging option. The orchestrator focuses on some steps and links with partners to carry out the rest. Capital requirements are lower than for the integrator, but some capital may be required for key processes not given out of the hand, like marketing. Capability requirements are the ability to collaborate with several partners simultaneously while not having direct control, complex project management skills, customer insight, brand management skills, a culture that can let go of certain areas while focusing on core competencies, an ability to move quickly—nimbleness.

Licensure requires hardly any capital and is the remedy for small companies, fast idea realization and for ideas out of the core business. The innovation is licensed to another company which takes it to the market. All expenses are born by the licensee. Capability requirements are intellectual-property management skills, basic research capabilities, contracting skills, and an ability to influence standards. Licensure is best used when there is strong intellectual property protection, the importance of innovator's brand is low, the market is new to the innovator, and significant infrastructure is needed but is not yet developed. The selection process of whether to integrate, orchestrate, or to license depends on the structure of the industry, the character of the innovation, and the risks to be taken. The following are the questions to be asked in the decision-making process:

- How familiar are we with the industry and its supply chains?
- Do we have the physical assets needed to enter the industry?
- Do we know the intensity of rivalry in the industry?
- What is the level of breakthrough of our idea?

- Can we handle all product components and the infrastructure required?
- Will the innovation work in a technical sense?
- Can the new product deliver the improved performance it promises?
- Customers may not buy the product even if it works. Is the improvement or the breakthrough exciting enough?
- Are substitutes around that shrink margins?
- What is the investment to commercialize the innovation?

Today's environments offer tremendous opportunities to shape formerly "unshapeable" industries and to design business models that are revolutionary. Traditional on-campus learning is more and more being substituted by sophisticated e-learning platforms. Untraditional providers take over protected markets in this field. The University of Phoenix, for instance, successfully competes with the state university system in Florida with a combination of on-site and internet-based learning. In 2001 two of IFEM's European partner schools jointly launched a global executive MBA program in cooperation with Florida Gulf Coast University (FGCU).[34] During the first year, the program was scheduled to be delivered on-site in Europe, complemented with nine e-based distance learning modules of basic business content. During the second year, five sessions were scheduled to be delivered both in Europe and in Florida and additional e-learning elements were to be used as an interactive platform and classroom. The program covers a geographical distance of over four thousand miles for most students. The real innovation was not the development of this e-based distance learning program, but the application of interactive language support (German, French, Spanish) within the courses. Most non-Anglo-Saxons are afraid of exposing themselves to English as a foreign language when immediate application in real business situations is requested (and your next educational milestone is real). We recommended that the European business schools and FGCU ease this gap by developing a multilingual learning platform. The introduced course material on the Web site was planned to be available in different languages such as German, French, and Spanish, which are first languages for many European students. Learning means communicating, and if educators and students openly communicate they will ultimately perform better. Where is the beef in the concept? Well, if translating from American English to German or Spanish works, it will work in any other language as well, for instance for the millions of Chinese students requiring management education in the future. The flip side of this revolutionary concept was that one administrator in Europe hindered the launch of the multilingual part of the program due to concerns of overcomplexity. He then isolated his major internal competitor from participating in the program and reduced his marketing base by half. The complexity certainly was a challenge to everybody involved and asked for 100 percent commitment—a concept difficult to translate into German. The project went back and forth for years and was stripped of its innovation to a classical MBA program. The market in Europe caught up, and today the offering is one of dozens of MBAs. In summer of 2004, our two partner schools were still waiting for the first class to be filled up. Many innovative ideas are slated to remain unrealized or not to bloom at their full potential just because the right partnership for realization cannot be found in time. One wimp can kill the fighting spirit of an army! When a project is ripe for realization you have to be able to take your shot right away. The window of opportunity may only be open for a short period of time. The key to such hunting instinct is an organization that is open and focuses on steering the customer relationship wherever the customer touches the organization.

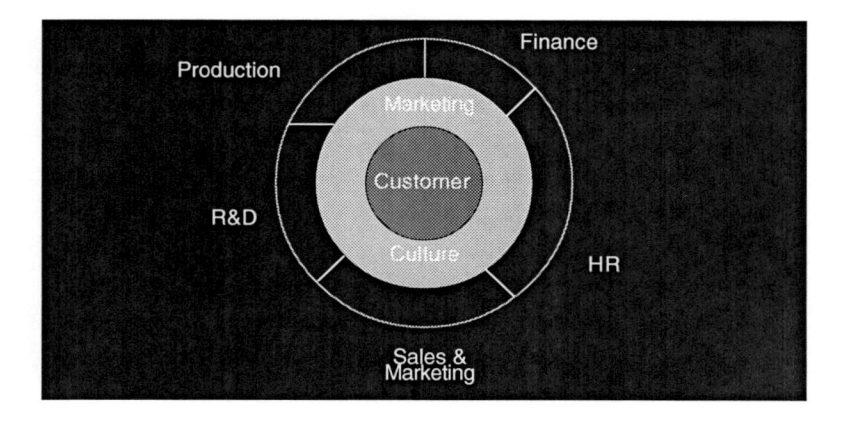

Figure 13: The Relationship Organization

Relationship organizations are customer centric. All entities simultaneously play their role in the customer relation and have real time access to databases required. Marketing is part of the culture and not only an organizational function. This organizational philosophy should not be confounded with organizations where the customer takes over control and terrorizes the company. Many of the original equipment manufacturers (OEMs) in the automotive industry or in telecommunication face this syndrome. One client I had manufactures high voltage switch gear. These are the switches that recognize irregularities in high voltage power flows and switch transformer plants off in a fraction of a second. These switches are required for power and light companies to have constant uptime. If the switches do not perform as scheduled or if there is a chain of negative events, blackouts occur. The performance of the switches depends on altitude and climate (humidity and temperature range). Our client was market leader in his field for years and beat larger companies like ABB and GE. The company was so customer focused that they developed regional lines of switch gears for every part of the world. In 1995 the company had over five hundred model platforms and a gross margin at about half the industry average. The reason for this lack of profitability was that high voltage switch gears have a product life cycle of fifty years. Due to the immense variety in the product range and the uniqueness of the regional systems, spare parts had to be manufactured at the time the original system was produced. The fact that the company basically produced every switch twice caused the gross margin to collapse because the spare parts were only billed to the customers when they were needed. Most of them were never needed, but stored for fifty years at the customer's power plant site. Total marketing focus is not customer focus either. From 1950 until the late 1960s many organizations were driven by marketing alone. The marketing guys were telling everybody what to do, and interestingly enough they were right most of the time, because the Western world was in the postwar growth mode. Until June 2004 Bauknecht, an appliance manufacturer and today a subsidiary of Whirlpool, successfully used the slogan "Bauknecht knows what women want!" in marketing. This sounds pretty overconfident to me today. Imagine this company's marketing perceived women so incapable of selecting their own appliances that Bauknecht had to make their choice for them.

ARE YOU "EASY TO DO BUSINESS WITH"?

A good test to check if you are "easy to do business with" (ETBW)[35] is to call the switchboard of your company, pretend you are a customer, and ask for yourself. Just let things happen from there. I am amazed by the responses people get with clients when they do this experiment out of a sales manager's office. Many times the sales VP recognizes that he/she is not even known as an employee of the corporation for which she has been working for years. Just recently, I tried to call the main number of a well-recognized educational degree equivalency accreditation agency in Miami. I actually wanted to return a call from the company's owner. Calling the main number, I was asked by the system to dial the extension of the person I wanted to speak with. All I wanted was to speak with the operator, as instructed by my contact, but the operator was not an offered option. Finally, after listening to different options for minutes, the system told me to "hold on" in order to "try that extension." It rang and rang and instead of the operator, I was finally connected to a voice mail. This blew my mind (and probably my voice), so I left a pretty rude statement about ETBW on that tape. I hung up, and it crossed my mind that my cell phone might have recognized the number with caller ID. With this feature I got directly back to the agency owner (to his total surprise). Every one of us has zillions of stories about experiences with not so "easy to do business with" organizations.

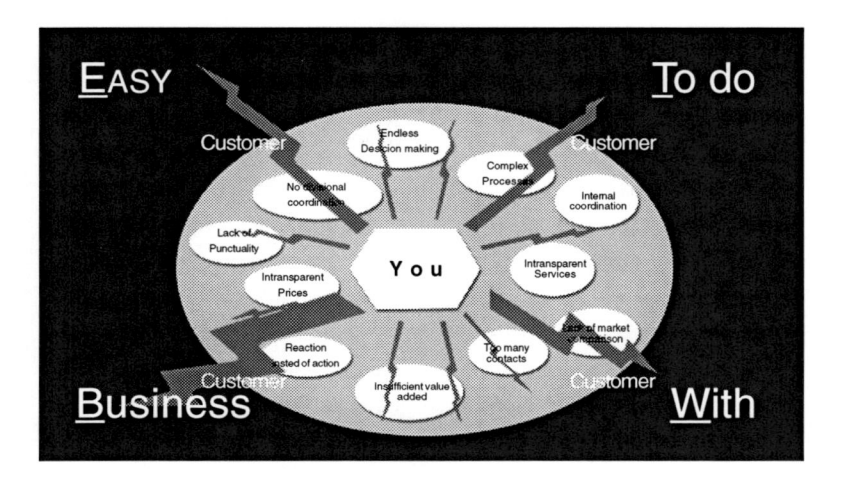

Figure 14: The ETBW Challenge

The concept, first described by Michael Hammer in his book *The Agenda*, is actually very simple:

You just have to have a single interface to each of your customers, offer adapted services for different customer segments, know what your customers are going to demand before they even know that they have a request, offer a seamless experience for your customers throughout all their request, let customers do more themselves, and measure the things that customers really consider to be important

Delta Airlines is a very good example of ETBW with their electronic travel initiatives, introduced in late 2002. Before this, Delta was not the best travel experience, but with the initiation of Delta's customer service initiatives, all of Hammer's requirements were fulfilled. The whole travel process can be managed online (one single interface); elite flyers and occasional flyers get distinguished services (adapted to segments); you print your boarding pass and there is no more standing in line for check-in (know what your customers want); booking and mileage statements are just a few clicks apart (seamless); you can handle everything from your desk (Delta let you do it yourself); and Delta gets instant data of your travel profile and even online comments about your satisfaction (measure). This all relates to the principle goal of ETBW: organizations are getting better and even lowering their costs, because they only do what customers pay for, or what the market perceives as a competitive advantage. ETBW is a business concept based on a different view of the value chain. Normally value chains are designed from the resource to the customer. I believe companies achieve a much-better understanding of the fulfillment of customer needs and demands if they design the value chain from the end-user (not necessarily the paying customer) of a product or service down the line to the resources or skills required for the first component of a product. If this perspective of the value chain is applied, an easy-to-do business with product or service is most often the outcome. I say "most often" because certain services are regulated, such as baggage screening at airports (which is certainly not always ETBW, but a necessity for homeland security).

Easy to Do Business With can very often be achieved with minimal steps. Instant check-in or express check-out at a hotel do not require a great deal of infrastructure or innovation, but these simple measures make your life as a traveler so much easier. If you get into a hotel that does not offer these standards, you consider them as antiquated. Running a business from the customer perspective seems to be obvious and simple. But running a business from the perspective of your customer's contacts is the real art of ETBW. Progressive insurance is such an example. Easter Saturday 2004 my son who is a student at the University of Miami came back home for a long weekend. He visited some friends in downtown Naples and had his car parked on a curb. The neighbor drove out of her driveway and backed into my son's car. She left a note and they met Easter Sunday to discuss the claim. The lady told my son that she would file a claim with her insurance company and that they would take care of the damages. It turned out that I was overly skeptical when I requested a police report. One hour after the lady and my son had adjourned their meeting we got a call from Progressive. Peter Lewis, CEO of Progressive, claims to sell speed, not insurance.[36] We got the proof that Easter Sunday. The Naples agent from Progressive asked us where we wanted to have the car repaired and as my son would be back at school Monday he scheduled repair at a body shop close to the University of Miami in Coral Gables. He even arranged a rental car for the duration of the repair (my son is nineteen years old and getting rental cars under the age of twenty-five is not that easy). Half an hour later the Progressive agent from Miami called and apologized that her colleague did not tell us the full story. They could offer my son's car to be picked up and returned directly at the university. This was a completely ETBW process and even made us forget that having a car repaired is usually a hassle.

TOP OF MIND

Imagine the chief information officer (CIO) of a midsize international corporation. The IT part of the organization needs to cope with growth and intends to buy new server or storage equipment. After thorough evaluation, three major suppliers of hardware have equivalent offers on the table. One of these suppliers is Big Blue (IBM), one is Sun, and the third is Hitachi. All make very good computers. Now the CIO presents the options to his colleagues on the board. Which provider will he propose, if he is a risk-conscious executive? The one that has the best or longest lasting reputation, of course, and that is, well, Big Blue. And it is on the top of our CIO's mind that "nobody has ever been fired for selecting IBM." If you are first in the mind of a potential customer, you have a good chance of getting the first call, and those suppliers who get the first call and do not screw it up will get the order.

There are four levels of top of mind: geographical, presence, image, and emotional. Geographical top of mind occurs when Bank of America has a branch every so many miles all along the coast of Southwest Florida, and the density makes you believe it is the only bank serving clients there (although there are many other banks around). Customers first select Bank of America for the convenience of a broad network. Then they experience extremely friendly customer service and an evolutionary concept of bank branches and start to love banking with this institution. When they enter the branch they are greeted and asked what kind of services they need. Plush leather chairs, widescreen TV, coffee, soft drinks, cookies, and books await customers in a loungelike environment. Closed offices allow them to conduct banking in privacy. The vault is automatic and works with a hand-reading device and pin. Several modern PC workstations allow customers to do online banking at the branch. Wherever they go in the United States, they will find a Bank of America branch and this completes the experience.

Starbucks Coffee is a very good example of top of mind through presence. They are always the coffee shop opening earliest at airports. Taking the 5.40 a.m. flight out of Fort Myers to Atlanta is biweekly chore of mine. As I walk into the awakening concourse at 4.30 a.m. a tempting aroma awakens me. Getting up the escalators there is this coffee shop with the green logo on the right and as a standard operating procedure I exchange $7 for a cup of Americano and a muffin before walking through security. Sixty percent of my fellow early bird passengers do the same.

Image top of mind can be positive or negative. An example of positive image is the IBM example as described above. A negative example would be the following: Having the traditional image of being the smartest cost cutters, the consultancy of McKinsey and Company had a hard time with their business after several high-rolling accounts went bankrupt[37] or had serious problems in the end of 2001. Their image, however, allowed them to recoup in a very short period of time.

Emotional top of mind is the most effective position you can have. Customers normally do not even consider looking for sources when they have an emotional relationship with a supplier. Such a relationship often comes from family ties or is based on friendship. Emotional top of mind can also be built over time. Swissair is a prime example. In most cases they were the only carrier Swiss business people would consider for travel, even if this meant unfavorable schedules or connections. It was all about this cozy feeling when boarding the plane.

As soon as you walked through the door of the plane you were greeted with a hearty *grüezi* and this made the Swiss feel straight at home. Swissair was also the only carrier where they could communicate in the unique Swiss dialect. For most companies, networks are the essential tool in building up emotional top of mind. European business people generally underestimate the value of personal and business networking. Fact is that for small businesses, this is the least expensive and most enduring marketing they can do. Once anchored in their communities, well-connected business people get quite an emotional top-of-mind effect and very loyal customers.

Fredrick Reichhelt[38] conducted a breakthrough study about the measurement of customer satisfaction or retention. Reichhelt states that the only way to grow profitable may lie in a company's ability to get its loyal customers to refer them and, in effect, to become its marketing department. Because customer referrals are the key, measuring and managing loyalty makes good sense. Traditional customer surveys measure a lot of things and are ineffective, because returns are traditionally low and customers do not like to respond to lengthy questionnaires. Across industries the following question was top ranking: "How likely is it that you would recommend [company X] to a friend or colleague?" Research shows that there is a strong correlation between a company's growth rate and the percentage of its customers who are promoting them, i.e., referring them to a friend or colleague. The study also shows that customers who do not actively refer a business can be detractors and therefore a threat. Therefore the net promoter base has to be measured. Net promoters are total promoters minus total detractors. On a scale of one to ten, ten means extremely likely to refer, five means neutral, and zero means "not at all likely." Promoters are customers with the highest rate of repurchase and referral and typically score a ten or nine on the scale. Actively and passively satisfied customers log eights and sevens respectively, but they are neutral in the referral behavior. Detractors normally score from zero to six. The interesting aspect of the study is that it neutralizes medium scoring and focuses on clear statements, positive or negative. Several industry-related studies delivered striking results comparing the correlation of three-year growth and net promoters. Southwest won the airline portfolio with over 50 percent net promoters and over five percent growth. MSN and Earthlink beat AOL in the Internet Service Provider battle with both over 25 percent growth and around 10 percent net promoters. Enterprise won the rental car race with over 12 percent growth and 33 percent net promoters. Both eBay and Amazon received net promoter scores of between 75 percent and 80 percent.

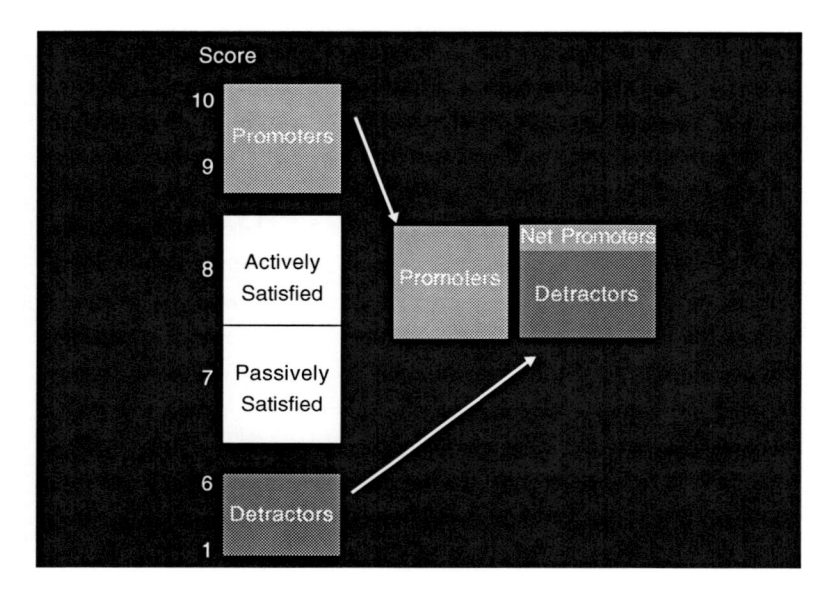

Figure 15: Top of Mind with Net Promoters

The net promoter methodology is actually not complicated. Survey a statistically valid sample of your customers with the following question: "How likely is it that you would recommend [brand or company X] to a friend or colleague?" It is critical to provide a consistent scale for responses that range from zero to ten, where zero means not at all likely, five means neutral, and ten means extremely likely. Resist the urge to let survey questions multiply; more questions diminish response rates along with the reliability of your sample. You only need one question to determine the status—promoter, actively satisfied, passively satisfied, and detractors. Calculate the percentage of net promoters.

Compare net promoter scores from segments and competitors (using the same survey method). Improve your score. Your benchmark could be eBay with a net promoter score of over 75 percent.

Once you know how many contacts within your target segments have what kind of relationship to you, you should tailor your marketing concepts around this knowledge. The next logical step would be to identify profitability of customer segments. A study from A. T. Kearney[39] shows that the traditional "ABC" Customer structure thinking should be revised and replaced with a "platinum," "gold," "silver," "bronze" and "tin" ranking. Ten percent of a company's customers are responsible for 30 percent of profits. These are the "platinum" patrons. The next 15 percent of the customer base, the "gold" customers, are responsible for 20 percent of profits. Platinum and gold together are 25 percent of the total customer base, and these two segments alone constitute 50 percent of all profits. A close look at satisfaction and net promoter rates of the first two tiers of the customer base is a must. Do you have enough contact to the best customers? Are your platinum customers satisfied and happy—how many active referrals did you get out of that precious base recently? Why are the gold customers really doing business with you? Is it because they are locked into your company for some reason, or is it because you are providing excellent products and services? How do you lever satisfaction of the gold segment? How is your management attention and sales force time allocated to the best part of the customer base? Catering platinum and gold customers is top management responsibility. Silver customers who make 35 percent of the customer base and a contribution of 40 percent to profitability should be catered just right—enough attention that they stay happy but with a business model where they are profitable at all times. The 20 percent bronze customers need a close look again, because they contribute only 5 percent of profit. Those bronze customers with silver potential should be pushed to become silver customers. Tin customers are another 20 percent of the customer base. They are high maintenance small accounts and can cost up to 15 percent of profitability due to their small size or complexity to serve. Once the customer base is thoroughly analyzed and clustered it needs a second thought and reflection. My consulting team and I faced this challenge at a major express parcel service provider in Poland. The client had clustered his customers into platinum, gold, silver, bronze, and tin and we were discussing the outcomes thoroughly at a workshop. We looked into each segment and talked about the future potential of each major account. The goal was to adjourn with a set of initiatives to launch shifts in the customer portfolio at the end of the session. Looking at the top five hundred companies in Poland we were astonished to find out that the client and the top five hundred portfolios were quite different. Many of the top five hundred companies were not even in an active relationship with our client. Consequently we established a set of target portfolios and merged them into the existing platinum, gold, silver, bronze, and tin clusters. As a result we got the preferred customer list and the relevant initiatives for the company.

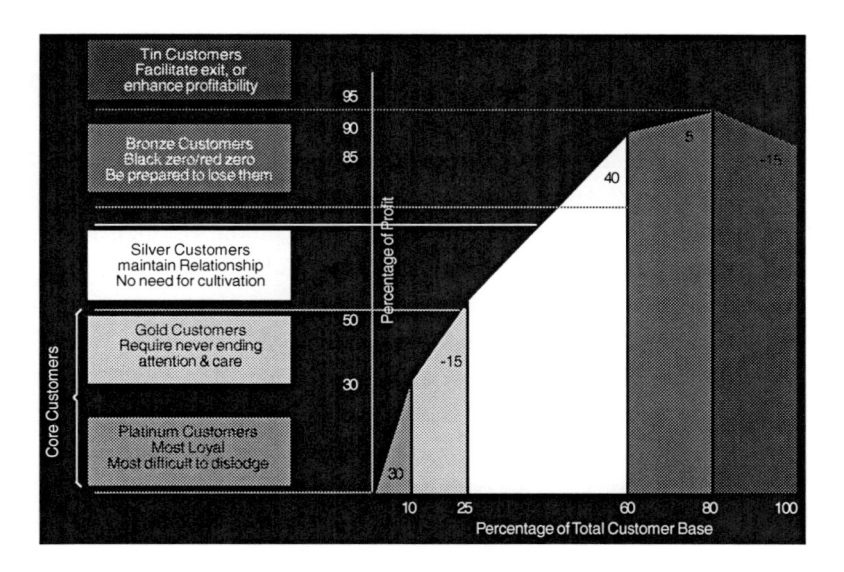

Figure 16: Customer Ranking

Top of mind is created top down. My experience shows that the larger the office of top managers, the less effective they are because they tend to hide themselves in their plush offices instead of exposing themselves to the harsh climate of the world of sales. Customer-focused organizations have their officers out at the front. Richard Branson, for example, regularly serves shifts as a flight attendant on his Virgin Atlantic airline in order to learn what customers want. Larry Bossidy[40] describes the execution style of a top executive concerned about top of mind of his company as banning the fat books and getting everybody to think and talk about reality. Ninety to ninety-five percent of an executive's schedule should be front related. A logical conclusion of this request is that executives basically do not need an office. From 1996 until 1999 I was the CEO of a large real estate development company in Germany that needed restructuring. The mandate was assigned to me following a consulting job at that public-private company and the contract allowed me to allocate time flexibly. When I came in the first day I found "my" office and "my" assistant waiting for me. My office comprised of nice oak furniture and was bigger than the living room at my house. Next to the office was a smaller meeting room with an oval table that seated eight. At noon that very first day I had that meeting room assigned to me for the time I was at headquarters—two hours a week. "My" office became the war room of the restructuring team and "my" assistant was shifted to her dream job in client services. I spend most of my time out at the front either with key accounts or with key enablers. This way I learned firsthand about the problems that lead the company into restructuring and understood the challenges we had. Before the company was driven by protocol and had a cover-your-back mentality. Execution was not on the agenda, sandbagging was the rule. We needed to change everything and rebuild the company from scratch. First, we had to bring customer segments and our organization in line. The rental apartment division with its thirty thousand subsidized and unsubsidized units had little difficulty to position itself top of mind, because they were the largest and least expensive provider of rental apartments in their market. Effectiveness and efficiency needed to be boosted, and quality levels of customer service needed to be enforced. The regional heads of the real estate development units had other challenges. Their main challenge was to get information on land that could be developed first. Top of mind meant to get the first phone call of a person or institution willing to sell a good property. After this, the processes had to be tailored to what we called "time to permit" to make the land owners and the investors happy. The city planning division however was dependent on getting planning contracts from districts, counties, and cities. Top of mind was created by cooperating with local universities who boosted our name in breakthrough studies and sometimes even unsolicited work. My role was to be the chief customer officer and to coordinate opportunities between the divisions to harvest synergies within our organization. The individual customer focus of every entity made them independent yet it also brought them together. We loosened the reins of operational leadership and delegated to the management whatever could be delegated. This again allowed us to view every entity as a business and finally lead to a split of the group and sale of the rental part. The results of the split allowed the owners to recoup their losses from a situation initially considered hopeless and to even get money out of it.

JUST DO IT

What a slogan! Nike rocked a decade with it. But it has so much merit. I remember a Nike[41] poster featuring Michael Jordan that hangs on my teenage daughter Deborah's bedroom wall: "I've missed more than 9000 shots in my career; I've lost almost 300 games; 26 times, I've been trusted to take the game winning shot, and missed; I've failed over and over and over again in my life—and that is why I succeed." Deborah is a first-generation immigrant kid and has made her way from shy "English as a second language" student to honor rolls and even top in her advanced placement English class. She probably has made every cultural mistake she could, and she had to "experience" her strategy throughout high school to get her a place as a Fulbright scholar at the Elliot School of international affairs at the George Washington University. Deborah had a strategy based on her key strengths or diligence, multicultural background and language talent and she wanted to get into this school and she got in. She knew that an Ivy League school would be a long shot and segmented her options accordingly. Execution is the discipline of getting things done.[42] It does not matter how many times you fail, as long as you are not running out of key resources or violate the law. When I was a consultant for Diebold we once took a survey about the number of strategies or concepts that were implemented more or less according to plan. The result was shocking: only 30 percent. From my experience, execution only works when the executive is out on the field. With growing size and globalization of organizations, another prerequisite comes into play: a culture that allows you to make mistakes and learn from them. While working in Europe, I often suffered from a no-mistake mentality, and this was actually one of several reasons to take advantage of my American citizenship and "move home." The worst experience I faced was with the ice cream division of a consumer goods manufacturer, where my assignment was to build up a chain of franchise ice cream parlors. The company had just acquired a major stake in an Italian chain of interstate restaurants and wanted to expand its consumer goods presence into these restaurants and their connected highway convenience shops. This was a spleen of the division head and everybody in the division knew that it had slim chances of working out: Italians do not eat Swiss ice cream, nor do they drink Swiss blend coffee. The division head did not care and we had to come up with a test market to prove that he was right. We assigned a project manager and this person had to prove in numbers that the project would be feasible. The report however indicated an immense amount of complexity and this was finally the reason to abandon a nonsense idea. Nobody made a mistake, everyone was always right. The no-mistake culture resulted in high costs and a project eventually going down the drain. Parallel, I was given the task of redesigning the ice cream parlor appearance worldwide. Most franchisees applauded the idea and were willing to invest in it. All we needed was a one-on-one model of the new concept. I had a small budget for agency work and mock-ups, but in the middle of the project the budget was cut without my knowledge. Without this information I pursued the project and when invoices of the agency remained unpaid, I learned that the budget had been stripped. No mock-up, no new concept. The division head drove it even further: "Mr. Stern, when can we see something tangible here?" I responded: "Sir, no budget, no results." I am sure you already know what the answer to this was: "I don't care how you do it!" This is not the meaning of "just do it." Nobody was willing to say "B" after having said "A."

The budget cut was the trick to avoid changes, and I would be the one blamed for failure, no matter what route I took: realize the project despite the budget cut, or stop it because it lacked funding. After a few more stomach-burning issues happened to me in that company, I just walked away from the job one day, and that was the best "just do it" feeling I have ever had. It changed my life because just a few days later, I started my career as a lecturer and consultant, and now I am even writing a book. Execution comes with empowerment, and empowerment requires a plan and resources to execute the plan. When we coach companies in execution of strategies, we always support our clients with tools to ensure that things are getting done. Flowcharts are a good way of visualizing a string of business administration tools required to formulate a strategy. The flowchart in figure 17 illustrates the roadmap to a market-oriented strategy (or marketing strategy). In the case below it is assumed that the normative elements of mission, the reason why a company has a right to exist, core values and vision do not need to be revised. In case that the project team concluded that mission, core values or vision needed an evaluation, they would just add these elements to the toolset.

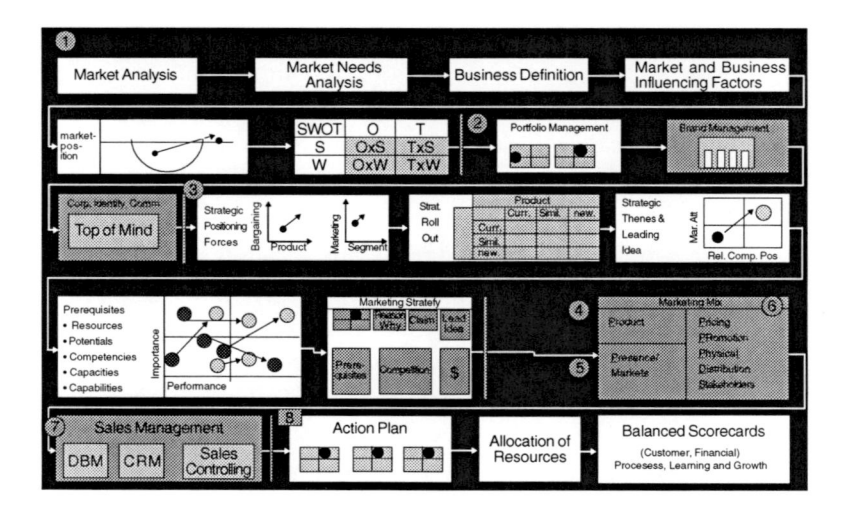

Figure 17: The Process of Formulating Market Strategies

Phase 1: Market Analysis and SWOT

The process starts with an analysis of the market and its environments. Market facts and market needs are looked at in an interactive process. The problem with market analysis is that there are no specific guidelines of how to conduct them. You basically start somewhere and dig deeper once you feel to have prospective information. The problem on basing analysis on statistics or public information is that your competitors have access to the same sources and certainly are not less professional than you in their conclusions. We tend to look out for alternative and even secondary sources of information. The ceoexpress.com[43] is a Web site that has been very helpful in this respect. The basic version is free and already an incredible wealthy source of guided information for the strategist and marketer. The premium version is even better, has more active content, and allows the user to tailor the site to his/her needs. Market analysis and market needs analysis should lead to the confirmation of the current business definition or show prospective new business definitions. A business definition is a clear statement from customer perspective what an organization is providing to its patrons. Virgin Atlantic who claims to be in entertainment, but at thirty thousand feet is not in the airline business—they are in entertainment. Virgin gives you the best business-class experience in the industry in their "Upper Class" (what a name!). Harley Davidson does not sell motor cycles. They "sell the ability for a forty-three-year-old accountant to dress in black leather, ride through small towns, and have people be afraid of him."[44] Harvard business school does not sell management education; they are in the business of providing their graduates the brightest perspectives in the world. Once you know your business definition you have to check if you have all market information for it. In most cases you will have to include data for more than one industry in your research. The key point during this phase is to be very open and not to miss an opportunity in creating something unique out of a business. Once the business definition is clear, all relevant factors influencing the business and the total environment of the business have to be explored. These are the same factors as described in chapter 4 earlier in this book. The analysis tasks are concluded by visualizing the competitive landscape on a chart where all competitors, their facts, their previous strategies, and their assumed directions are noted. We very often use an adapted version of Porter's curve[45] for this. Figure 18 describes the landscape of the American textile chemical industry in 2002 and clearly shows that the proponent company (we) only had two options: to get right through the line of scrimmage between competitors E and D, or to refocus on profitability and shift to the upper left.

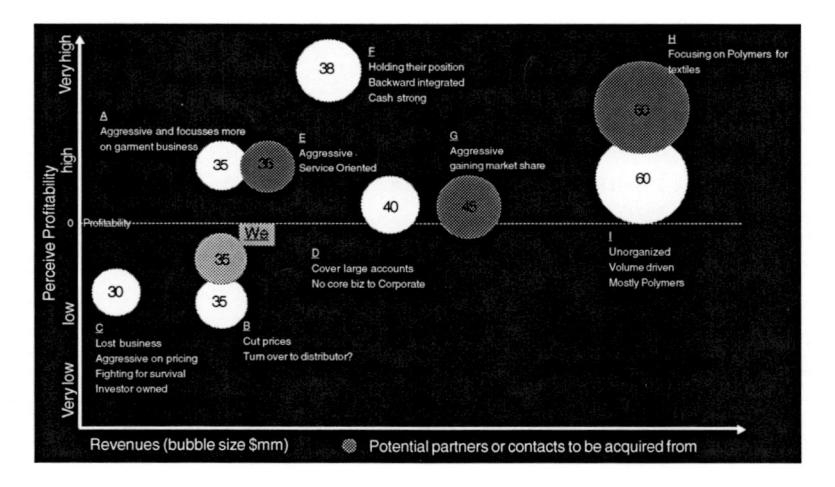

Figure 18: Competitive Landscape

At the end of the analysis process, all external information collected should allow an assessment of opportunities and threats. All internal information gathered should make it possible to define strengths and weaknesses. The methodology to apply is commonly known as the SWOT matrix. Researching for this book, I could not find a clear reference whom to credit for this methodology, but my opinion is that it is widely misused, with or without consultants. Traditionally people gather for a SWOT workshop and brainstorm with a coach in front of a flipchart. The strongest brainstormers get their points on the flipchart, the slower thinkers do not. The result is a list of strengths, weaknesses, opportunities, and threats that merely delivers input to the strategy documents. Most of the time people remember those workshops as nice but not very useful exercises. I developed a different process during my consulting practice and also registered it for a U.S. copyright in 2003.[46] It is very simple to make a striking tool out of a SWOT. First, all participants of the project team should get an e-mail with a short explanation what is going to be done and of course the notification that their brains are going to be picked. The project leader sends a set of forms like in figure 19 and asks the team to list each strengths, weaknesses, opportunities, and threats on a simple form like in figure 19. We already ask the delegates to give an opinion on what every listed item would mean for the strategy (conclusions).

Strenghts	Implications for the Strategy

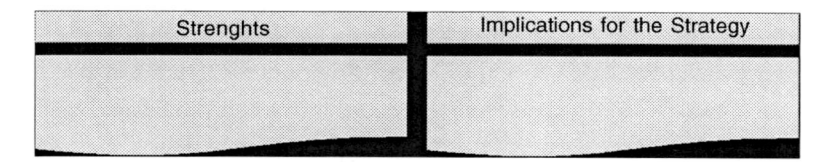

Figure 19: Initial SWOT Assessment Form

Participants normally get these forms on a Thursday and are requested to respond by the following Tuesday. As there is a weekend in between the days, there is enough time for everyone to massage their thoughts. We then collect all returns and eliminate overlaps. A new list is established where all SWOTs are mentioned with all remarks for each item listed. This list should now be numbered in alphabetic manner, similar to strength A, strength B, etc. On Thursday the delegates get another e-mail with the new SWOT list and all conclusions/remarks. They are now requested to rank each category with points. They can give three points to the item in each category they find most important, two points to the number two, and one point to number three. Responses are again due by the following Tuesday, but this time a simple e-mail will be enough. It could look like this: "Strengths: C=3, D=2, E=1, Weaknesses: A=3, F=2, H=1, etc." This participant would have ranked strength C as the most important one, strength D as his number two, and strength E as his number three. The project leader collects all emails and establishes a new list with rankings for each category. The remarks/conclusions are carried forward on the ranked list per category. It may very well be that certain items get the same amount of points and therefore ex-equo rankings. It is also very probable that certain items do not get any points, and they are just listed at the end of each category ranking. This intermediary result is already better than what you can get out of most of the SWOT flipchart exercises, because each item has conclusions for the strategy remarked from the perspectives of every single participant. The ranked list now becomes the basis for future work and should be sent out together with the invitation for the first SWOT workshop with the team. First item on the agenda is a discussion of the rankings to come to conclusions and to identify initiatives that can be launched without prejudice for the future. Such items will most probably be found in the nonranked sections of the lists. The focus on the lists is now reduced to the top three items each and they should be discussed in detail and agreed upon by all participants. At this point the coach starts working on strategic initiatives. With forms like in figure 20, the following reflections are made: opportunities with strengths, opportunities with weaknesses, threats with strengths, and threats with weaknesses.

		Opportunities
	• O1: • O2: • O3:	
Strenghts		Option Generator
• S1 • S2 • S3	O1/S1: O1/S2: O1/S3:	
	O2/S1: O2/S2: O2/S3:	
	O3/S1: O3/S2: O3/S3:	
	All O/S1: All O/S2: All O/S3:	
	O1/All S: O2/All S: O3/All S:	

Figure 20: Option Generator

If the external analysis has been done properly, all opportunities and threats should be known and assessed. If the internal analysis has been done properly, all strengths and weaknesses have been recorded and evaluated properly. Therefore, all potential outcomes should be looked at in the methodology. The team works with four different views during the process. A very optimistic optic compares opportunities and strengths. In our practice we humoristically call this a "Bill Gates Perspective," because all people at Microsoft are very optimistic and the company just rides on a positive wave. An opportunistic optic weighs opportunities against weaknesses to find out what needs to be done so that weaknesses do not jeopardize opportunities. A cautious perspective evaluates what the options are when threats meet strengths. We call this the "Andy Grove" perspective, based on his book *Only the Paranoid Survive*.[47] According to Grove almost anything can create a Strategic Inflection Point, the nightmare moment every leader dreads. Finally, every business needs to evaluate their worst case and what to do to prevent it. The worst case occurs when threats are levered by weaknesses. This is commonly called the moment when Murphy's law hits a company. The following is an excerpt from a magazine article I found on the Web:[48] Murphy's law ("If anything can go wrong, it will") was born at Edwards Air Force Base in 1949 at North Base. It was named after Capt. Edward A. Murphy, an engineer working on Air Force Project MX981, (a project) designed to see how much sudden deceleration a person can stand in a crash. One day after finding that a transducer was wired wrong, he cursed the technician responsible and said, "If there is any way to do it wrong, he'll find it." The contractor's project manager kept a list of "laws" and added this one, which he called Murphy's law. Actually, what he did was take an old law that had been around for years in a more basic form and give it a name. After these reflections the SWOT can be finalized and the business has to decide what strategic focus it is going to have. As all external and all internal criteria of the business have been considered, the project team can just pick their options out of one, or several boxes, depending on their strategy focus.

	Opportunities • O1 • O2 • O3	Threats • T1 • T2 • T3
Strengths • S1 • S2 • S3	Strengths + Opportunities • Optimistic Strategy Focus: "Bill Gates"-type strategies: Focus on future and oppurtunities forget the past and hope to outplace the environment	Strengths + Threats • Paranoid Strategy Focus: "Andy Grove"-type strategies: Always watch the radar screen for threats and never trust the sustainability of your strenghts
Weaknesses • W1 • W2 • W3	Weaknesses + Opportunities • Opportunistic Strategy Focus: Oppurtunities outweigh all disadvantages and you hope to succeed despite your weaknesses	Weaknesses + Threats • Risk adverse Strategy Focus: "Murphy"-type strategies: Expect the worst case at the least favorable time and prevent risk at all means

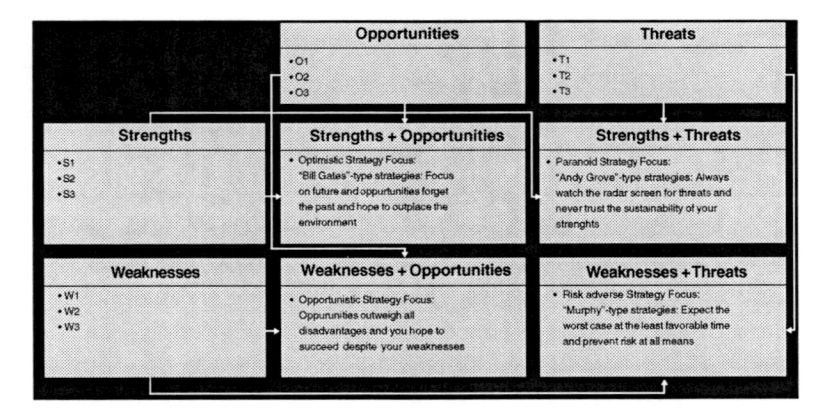

Figure 21: SWOT Decision Matrix

Phase 2: Portfolio Management

In many cases we already know what to do after the SWOT. Sometimes we need further evidence and want to look at additional tools. So we start working on our business portfolios and decide how resources should be allocated to the various segments or business fields. We have to ask ourselves questions about the use of brands and how communication budgets should be distributed to the brands. The majority of our work has already been done with the SWOT, so this phase should not take too much time. I am not a big proponent of classical portfolios comprised of axes with several weighted criteria each. In my perspective, such portfolios cannot be more than decision-supporting tools, because the complex process of building the block of criteria and weighting them can be influenced or even unwillingly steered into the wrong direction. One case I experienced was a precious metal manufacturing and trading company with fifty-two business units. Their portfolio management manual was professionally designed by the head of strategic planning, a very bright former McKinsey and Company consultant. I was in charge of training their first-year management level in weekly strategy and marketing brush-ups and used the company's business administration tool to explain newest theory and its application in practice. We commented on their business portfolio and discussing the various positions, the class came to an astonishing finding: for over three years they made decisions based on an initial portfolio manual that weighted market growth and market share by each thirty percent as criteria for market attractiveness. The problem was that two years earlier corporate management had decided that not growth and market share but profitability of a market was the driver of the strategy, but nobody ever adapted the portfolio management manual. So the company actually got rid of business units not positioned favorably on their portfolios, and they proudly explained that in most of the cases they could convince the local business unit management for a management buyout. No wonder, whenever the local management realized that their businesses were hidden gems but were not positioned favorably in the strategy sessions they just waited for the call from corporate to close the operations. Then they took the businesses over for next to nothing, went on with business as usual, and made a fortune in no time. In some cases they even sold the business back to the corporation after a while. If you use portfolios, I recommend that you use axes that are clearly defined by one criterion each and draw portfolios with the two axes and the bubble size as the third dimension. This approach is measurable and simple. Also, it is supported by Microsoft Excel and other office applications. After the portfolio issue is clarified, you have to decide what your brand(s) can do for your portfolio bubbles. Brands can virtually be the turbocharger of a portfolio bubble. My experience is that companies either are challenged with not enough brands or with too many brands. Very few businesses have just the right mix. Differentiation, relevance, esteem, and knowledge are the four elements commonly recognized as drivers of a brand.[49] A brand has to base differentiation to become relevant to a certain population in the market. This relevance builds esteem and people start paying a premium for the brand and more and more people remember the brand and perceive it necessary in the market place. Playing with these four levers is costly, and therefore, a business should focus its communication resources on the brands with the highest potential. This is where we commonly measure marketing return on investment.[50] The idea is to invest marketing funds where it makes most sense. We normally propose a process comparing differentiation, efficiency, placement costs and complexity of a brand as outlined in figure 22.

78   CHRIS J. STERN

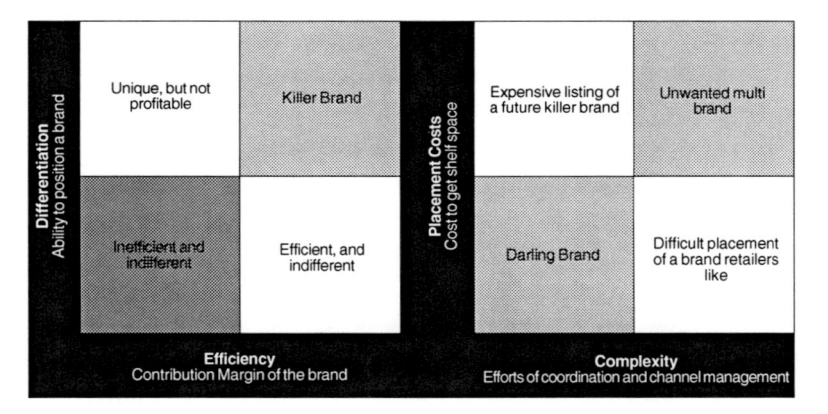

	Unique, but not profitable	Killer Brand		Expensive listing of a future killer brand	Unwanted multi brand
Differentiation Ability to position a brand	Inefficient and indifferent	Efficient, and indifferent	**Placement Costs** Cost to get shelf space	Darling Brand	Difficult placement of a brand retailers like
	Efficiency Contribution Margin of the brand			**Complexity** Efforts of coordination and channel management	

Figure 22: What Brands to Invest In

Phase 3: Crafting the Strategy

Every business unit or segment now needs to be positioned strategically. Figure 23 explains the basic methodology of positioning. The four elements that drive a business unit are product power, bargaining power, marketing power, and segment power. Product power refers to the performance of the product or service offered in the business unit or segment.

BargainingPower (Ability to offer the better bargain)	better	Lower performance but cheaper	Cheaper but better	Cheaper and better	Unique and inexpensive	**Marketing Power** (power and influence in the markets)	high	Push into a tough market	Full stream to gain market share	Full steam to take it all
	similar	Lower performance at same price	Same performance same price	Better performance same price	Unique at the same price		average	Not enough budget in tough market	Adequate to maintain market share	Hot market and enough maketing
	Lower	More expensive and worse	More expensive and similar	More expensive but better	Superb but expensive		Low	Now budget in though market	Low budget in difficult market	Hot market needs little marketing
		Worse	similar	better	unique			Low	average	high
		Product Power (Advantages in Performance)						**Segment Power** (Sufficient customers with sufficient Demand)		

Figure 23: Strategic Positioning

If a product or service is unique or really special it can be an easy sell and does not need to be pushed with a low price. If a product or service is commoditized, price is an issue, and the competitor with the highest gross margin will have the biggest bargaining power, because he can lower the price more than his direct competitors and still make a gross profit. Hence, the first step in positioning is to define how much product power is required to succeed in the sectors or markets targeted and to identify how sensible these markets are to prices. The ideal position of course would be to have a superior product with very low costs of goods sold and a high selling price. In a second portfolio the same product or service needs to be positioned comparing segment power and marketing power. Marketing power refers to the funds available to promote a product or service. Segment power is the ability of a company to trigger demand either by segmenting specifically or by finding markets with a lot of purchasing will and purchasing power. Again the ideal positioning would be finding markets or segments that are hot to buy while simultaneously having abundant marketing funds available. The positioning work explores all four criteria in detail and compares the business against its direct rivals on each axis and within both portfolios. To do so the criteria to define product power, bargaining power, marketing power, and segment power need to be found first. Our experience shows that four to five criteria for each axis are sufficient. Product power for example could consist of product quality, performance advantages, design, and convenience. Criteria for bargaining power could be price point, margin, transaction costs, and access to resources. Common criteria for marketing power are budget, number of sales associates, aggressiveness, performance at point of sales, and channel penetration. Top of mind, market share, market penetration, market size, and loyalty of accounts are the criteria commonly taken to define segment power. Comparison of the business unit against competitors is done in a simple grid scaled lower, comparable, better, and excellent, where lower gets one point, comparable two points, better three points, and excellent gets four points. Each criterion is measured against competitors and the position on the portfolio axis is the total of points achieved versus the potential maximum of points. With four criteria defining an axis the maximum of points and the top position on an axis would be sixteen. One of the most common mistakes in marketing is that businesses do not take competitive reaction into consideration. This simple methodology prevents that common flaw and also allows the marketer to define what he/she intends to do on each axis if action items underline the movement on every axis. The relevant question during the process will be "how would our competitor react if we do this or that?" We get excellent results when clients agree to have at least one team playing the competitor and compare the findings of the opposing team with their own conclusions. If this war game is played diligently, the outcome is a set of scenarios, and the strategists get a better understanding of how a market would react to competitive moves.

Although we should now have a good understanding of potential strategies and competitive moves, we have not yet considered the dynamic dimensions product and market rollout. Back on the overall business level, all segments should now be compared in terms of what markets are tackled when and what product or service enhancements are added at what point. The basic methodology for this step was first published by Igor Ansoff[51] in an article called "Strategies for Diversification" in the *Harvard Business Revue* in 1957 and is commonly called the product/market matrix. The output of the tool is a series of suggested growth strategies that set the direction of the business. If a business focuses on selling existing products in existing markets, market penetration is the suggested strategy. Market development is the name given to a growth strategy where the business seeks to market its existing products into new markets. Product development is the name given to a strategy where the business aims to introduce new products into existing markets. Diversification is a growth strategy where a business markets new products in new markets. Probability of success and resources required to succeed vary widely between those four generic strategies. Market penetration has the highest success rate and requires fewest resources. Market development and product development need four to eight times the resources of market penetration and have a probability of success of about 50 percent. Diversification needs ten to twelve times the resources of market penetration and has a probability of success of only 10 percent. Resource ratios and success rates depend on industry sector and market. We found in our practice that Ansoff's matrix could be enhanced by taking a third element into account. Many times the terms existing and new were too digital for us. What if a business enters markets that are somewhat related? A German business trying to enter the Austrian and Swiss markets, for example, can rely on the same language and some cultural overlaps. It does not need to translate sales materials and can use the same call center for supportive services. The complexity for this business is far lower in Austria and Switzerland than if it tried to enter the U.S. markets, because the new European markets are related. The same applies to products. If a business is enhancing a product line or adding new features, this could lead to related fields or solutions. When Gillette added its electrical razor M3Power to its Mach 3 product line it did not venture into a completely new product. Gillette had extensive experience in hygienic electronics from its Braun Oral B toothbrush line. Risks of the new product line were controllable, and customer needs were understood. The microrazor was a related product. Figure 24 shows the adapted product/market matrix as we currently use it to explore risks and complexity of a business.

	Exsisting Products/ Technology →	Related Products/ Technology →	New Products/ Technology
Existing Markets/ Function ↓	Positioning Strategy	Flanking Strategy	New Strategy
Related Markets/ Function ↓	Broadening Strategy	Repositioning Strategy	Remarketing Strategy
New Markets/ Function	BSpin-Off Strategy	Remarketing Strategy	Diversification Strategy

Figure 24: Strategic Rollout Matrix

It is important to visualize strategic risk exposure by comparing the rollout strategies of all business units or segments in one chart. The best way to do this is to enter the business units and their perceived strategies over time as bubbles into a rollout chart as in figure 24. Every quadrant shows the generic strategy required to succeed in each situation. Positioning is penetrating existing markets with existing products. Flanking strategies are selected to launch related products in existing markets. New products in existing markets need new strategies. Existing products in related markets need a broadening strategy. A business adding related products and expanding into related markets will need to reposition itself. New products in related markets need a new segmentation, hence a remarketing strategy. Spin-offs are a very efficient way to market existing products in completely new markets, because the spun-off business does not rely on traditional rules and roles. Related products in new markets again call for resegmentation or remarketing. New products in new markets are a traditional diversification.

Once the rollout reflections are made, the company can summarize its options and formulize the strategy. This is usually a filtering process and may include compromises driven by resources or facts. The influencing factors as described in chapter 4 (figure 10) should be revisited and used as the strategic controlling tool. Resources and competencies required should be assessed in terms of where the business stands and what it needs for the strategy. Finally the strategy should be summarized on one page. The more focused the better. One of the best examples of a strategy that can basically be laid out on the back side of a business card can be found at the Web site of TietoEnator[52] and is illustrated in figure 25 below.

A strategy like that can easily be explained to every person in a business. Remarks to guiding principles can be put on the company Web site as references for employees and partners alike. TietoEnator's strategic framework is actually uncomplicated and it is very well explained. TietoEnator's mission is "building the information society." They are fulfilling their mission by consulting, developing, and hosting their

```
                    ┌─────────────────────────┐
                    │   The world leading     │
                    │   high value added      │
   Vision           │   IT services provider  │
                    │   in selected verticals │
         ┌──────────┴─────────────────────────┴──────────┐
         │              Growth 20%                        │
         │              Profit over 10%                   │
   Goals │              Preferred employer                │
         └──────────┬─────────────────────────┬──────────┘
                    │   Global leverage of    │
                    │   vertical expertise    │
   Strategy         │   Solutions             │
                    │   Partnerships          │
         ┌──────────┴─────────────────────────┴──────────┐
         │       Building the Information Society         │
   Mission└──────────┬─────────────────────────┬──────────┘
                    │   Customer Benefit      │
   Values           │   Personal Growth       │
                    └─────────────────────────┘
```

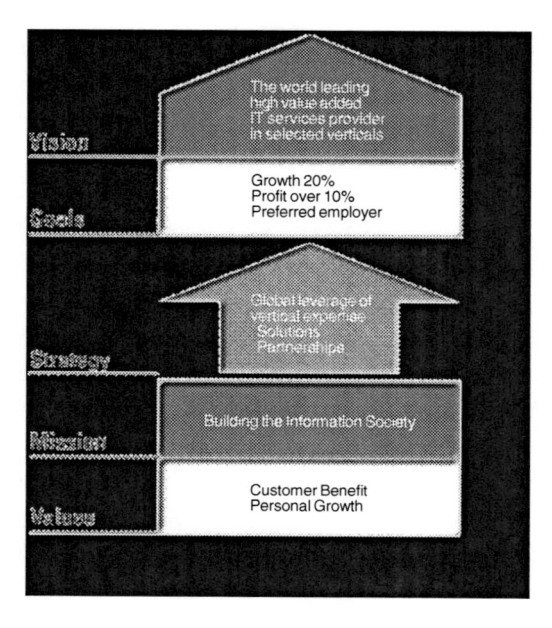

Figure 25: One-Page Strategy

customers' digital businesses. Their vision is to become the world's leading provider of high-value-added IT services in selected vertical markets. Leading in their thinking means leadership in expertise, market share, and profitability. High-value-added means high leverage and profitability for both their customers and themselves. TietoEnator's transformation is characterized by the following trends: higher up in the value chain, deeper into the core verticals, and further into the global market.

TietoEnator's long-term objectives are top-line growth over 20 percent, organic growth at least in pace with market growth, additional growth through acquisitions, operating profit margin (EBIT) to exceed 10 percent; each business area to create shareholder value, to be the employer preferred by IT professionals.

TietoEnator is positioning itself against its competitors in segments of the market where it can maintain superior expertise, strong market position, and solid profitability.

Their focus and differentiation originates from their background and customers. TietoEnator focuses on vertical markets that represent the strongest Nordic industries and deepest accumulated expertise of the company. In these high-priority vertical markets, TietoEnator has the capacity to assume comprehensive and continued responsibility for IT functions, acting as an enhanced IT department for its customers. They call this kind of relationship an IT partnership. Within the same verticals TietoEnator is refining its expertise further into repeatable solutions comprising concepts, components, and ready-made products. These repeatable solutions represent the most crystallized form of their vertical expertise. The strong vertical focus leads them to two types of services: customer partnerships and repeatable solutions. In customer partnerships their scope is Nordic, in repeatable solutions it is global. To achieve its long-term financial targets, TietoEnator aims to be the preferred IT partner for Nordic clients and the best solutions provider globally in defined core applications in selected verticals. The areas with most potential for global growth are banking and finance, telecom and media, and forest, targeting net sales growth over 20 percent. Healthcare and energy will aim at very strong regional development while other businesses will strive for growth at least at the pace of the market. Growth investments like acquisitions will be targeted at strengthening TietoEnator's capabilities for solution partnerships in new markets.

TietoEnator profiles itself as a highly professional European IT services company with a strong Nordic background. Their values are customer benefit and personal growth. All their work reflects a strong commitment to creating added value for their customers and giving their people the continuous opportunity to grow and develop as individuals and as team members.

Phases 4 to 6: Marketing Mix

The term marketing mix was coined by Neil H. Borden in 1964,[53] but it was Philip Kotler who made the term famous in his 1970's standard work *Marketing Management*.[54] Traditionally the mix was defined as product, place, price, and promotion. Several scholars added more *P*s, but the basic idea of the marketing mix as description of the detailed tactics per segment per market remains. We usually work with six *P*s that we divide into three groups: product, place, price, promotion, physical distribution, and politics. Product is a group for itself, and so is place. Products have to be accepted in the places they should be sold in. If this is not the case, a product will normally fail. As every market differs from another, price, promotion, physical distribution, and management of politics and stakeholders have to be tailored to every company. Going through the process of strategy formulation, the marketing mix should not be too difficult. Most of the groundwork to design the marketing mix has already been conducted during the strategic positioning (phase 2) and can just be taken over. The next steps have to be done for each segment or business unit individually and this is where the busy works starts. The whole process of strategy formulation is designed to avoid mistakes resulting in costly busy work having to be redone, so you should be confident at this point that you are positioned properly. In phase 4 we describe in detail the product and service from customer perspective.

This starts with a description of how customer needs and channel needs will be addressed and explores how customer desires and channel desires could be satisfied in the future. The efficiency of a segment is determined by describing its expected performance within the horizontal product range (broadness). Effectiveness of a business unit is its scheduled performance within a vertical of the product range, i.e., how it competes against its direct rivals in a group of products. The role of technology in a segment needs to be illustrated, especially in segments with significant vulnerability. Then product design and the reaction to it should be described from the perspectives of every user and also nonusers like stakeholders or competitors who could get in touch with the product. It may make sense to visualize the results of this step with comic-type drawings. A similar approach should be taken for the evaluation of the brand value from the perspective of all potential users and stakeholders. Finally the life cycle position of the segment needs to be measured and compared with its peer segments.

In phase 5, information from phase 2 and from the strategic rollout is translated into tangible tactics for markets and places. A visualization of market segmentation should be followed by discussion about the aggressiveness a business intends to use to gain or maintain market share in existing, related, and new markets. A product needs to be positioned differently in each market, because the rules for each market are so different. Ries and Traut [55] researched positioning intensively and came to the conclusion that companies should always try to achieve leadership positions in a selected vertical. If a product is not going go be first in a market, the company marketing must find an unoccupied position where it can lead. Speed and market knowledge are the keys. Mitsubishi Motors learned this the hard way when they introduced the first generation of their Pajero sport utility vehicle in May 1985.[56] The Pajero was a perfect SUV for the Latin American markets and one of the most cited marketing flops ever. It had breakthrough standard equipment like front-wheel independent suspension, turbo diesel engine, center-through drive train, and automatic free-wheel. Sales were appealing as long as the vehicle was marketed in non-Spanish speaking areas. In the Latin markets, sales flopped and probably prevented Mitsubishi from taking over a leading market share from Jeep, Nissan, and Toyota. The reason for failure was a simple omission to look up the word in any better Spanish dictionary. *Pajero* refers to a person who satisfies himself sexually and certainly is no word a Latino would like to have as a reference on the back of his car. Subsequently Mitsubishi needed to correct the name of the car to "Montero" for the Latin American markets.

In phase 6 a detailed business concept including pricing, promotion, physical distribution, politics, and stakeholders should be designed per market. Markets have different price floors and price ceilings and are different in terms of what pricing to select. The four basic types of pricing are cost-based pricing, competitor-reference pricing, value-based pricing, and enhanced pricing. For cost-based pricing, fixed and variable costs are determined, and then bottlenecks and constraints are pinpointed. The desired margin and discount policies are developed after analyzing inventory, quick response, and forecast error rates. For competitive pricing, the life cycle position needs to be determined before assessing competitor products and services. The price is set after evaluating switching costs of customers. For value-based pricing an economic model of the customer's business is designed first. The bottom-line impact of the products or services for the customer have to be determined to outline a business case for each account based on a desirably high price. Enhanced pricing is based on added features or services. Bundled solutions based on a determination of what customers' value are priced after an assessment of performance and reliability requirements.

The key contents for the promotion concept for each market should be filtered out of the strategic positioning (chapter 2). Many brands dilute a company's ability to be a successful and powerful communicator in multiple markets. Focus on few brands per market potentially is a better approach for successful promotion, if the promotional activities are tailored to the tastes and expectations of the customers in a market. The world's largest realtor, RE/MAX real estate started 1973 with twenty-one associates. It had 4,730 offices with 87,325 associates in 47 countries in 2003 and estimates to have over 130,000 associates in 2007.[57] There is one common logo (the balloon) in promotion, but the franchise religiously adapts itself to the distinguished promotional needs of every market. Local country franchises like Switzerland sponsor local athletes and local events—because the Swiss people would never do business with a realtor they perceive not to be Swiss. Germany, for example, has five local editions (Central, East, Northwest, Southwest, and Bavaria) with distinctive offerings based on a common platform. This makes promotion an effective local contributor in an efficient way.

The definition of a physical distribution concept does not need a lot of reflection in most cases. Most markets just have their rules and if a business is not strong, or segmented enough to change them, it has to comply to this imperative. In American community banking, for example, the requirement is to be within one and a half miles of the customer for a checking account relationship.[58] Customers only accept longer distances to deposit their checks if they get really different services.

Although it may sound strange for non-American readers, checking is still the most common form of money management in the United States and despite its complexity it has its merits, because there is immediate proof and a paper trail of the transfer. A bank can only be successful in the United States if it offers drive-through windows for banking in the neighborhood of its target clients. In every city larger bank corporations like Bank of America, Fleet Boston, and Wachovia fight each other on the same intersection with nice-looking bank branches. Smaller community banks therefore need to tailor their offerings to their realistic geographical outreach and then relentlessly focus on relationship banking.

Politics and stakeholders are the sixth element of the marketing mix, and they require presidential attention. Many companies underestimate the influence of stakeholders on their businesses. Potential business stakeholders are government, employees, owners, community, and consumers. Stakeholders could be defined as individuals and groups with a multitude of interests, expectations, and demands as to what the business should provide to society; or in short, anyone who is able to sweeten the cake or to spoil the soup. A stake is an interest or a share in an undertaking and can be interest, right, or ownership. Any individual who possesses a stake is a stakeholder. From the political environment these could be federal, state, or local agencies. From the community stakeholders are the general public, environmental groups, and civic groups. Employee stakeholders are minorities, women, older employees, unions, and other activists. Owner stakeholders are private investors, institutional groups and board members. Consumer stakeholders come from average consumers, product liabilities, and social activists. Primary stakeholders are those who have a stake in the organization and its success, secondary stakeholders are those that have a public or special interest stake in the organization. Core stakeholders are essential to the survival of the business. Strategic stakeholders are vital to the organization and the opportunities and threats it faces. Environmental stakeholders are all others in the business' environment. Stakeholders may have a legitimate claim, the power, capacity or ability to produce an effect, or urgency in the degree to which their claim demands immediate attention. Stakeholders first need to be identified and then clustered into a portfolio with the axes stakeholder's potential for threat to the organization and stakeholder's potential for cooperation. Next, the question what the stakeholders' stakes are needs to be answered. Reflection should be given to the opportunities and challenges presented by the stakeholders and to what economic, legal, ethical, and philanthropic responsibilities the firm has. Strategies or actions to manage stakeholder responsibilities must then be developed. The most important stakeholders need to be catered by the board or the senior management of an organization. For every potential influential stakeholder the company should establish and follow through on a written concept. This includes answering the questions, should the firm deal directly or indirectly with stakeholders? Should it take the offense or the defense in dealing with stakeholders? Should it accommodate, negotiate, manipulate or resist stakeholder overtures? Should it employ a combination of the above strategies or pursue a singular course of action? The seven metaprinciples for stakeholder management were developed by Max Clarkson between 1993 and 1998.[59] They encourage and require management to more specific stakeholder principles and then to implement those in accordance with the seven principles. Principle 1 states that managers should acknowledge and actively monitor the concerns of all legitimate stakeholders and should take their interests appropriately into account in decision-making and operations. Principle 2 tells managers should listen to and openly communicate with stakeholders about their respective concerns and contributions and about the risks that they assume because of their involvement with the corporation. Principle 3 suggests that managers should adopt processes and modes of behavior that are sensitive to the concerns and capabilities of each stakeholder constituency. Principle 4 emphasizes that managers should recognize the interdependence of efforts and rewards among stakeholders, and should attempt to achieve a fair distribution of the benefits and burdens of corporate activity among them, taking into account their respective risks and vulnerabilities. Principle 5 says that managers should work cooperatively with other entities, both public and private, to insure that risks and harms arising from corporate activities are minimized and, where they cannot be avoided, appropriately compensated. Principle 6 advocates that managers should altogether avoid activities that might jeopardize inalienable human rights (e.g., the right to live) or give rise to risks which, if clearly understood, would be patently unacceptable to relevant stakeholders. Principle 7 says that managers should acknowledge the potential conflicts between (a) their own role as corporate stakeholders, and (b) their legal and moral responsibilities for the interests of stakeholders, and should address such conflicts through open communication, appropriate reporting, and incentive systems and, where necessary, third party review.

Phase 7: Sales Management

Sales management is translating strategies into tangible results at the customer front. Tangible results should be a high conversion rate of sales calls, closed and cashed deals in the stretch goal mark, increased market share, acceptable retention rates per segment, and beyond-average return on sales investment. It always shocks me when European executive-class students tell me that it is common that sales people do not know the strategy of the company and in many cases are not even given insight into calculation of their products and services. Often sales people are on the bottom line of the appreciation scale of a firm. People who "do the real work" perceive that the sales guys who make a lot of money with little work. Sales management is more than herding a group of outgoing people with a leash. By bringing a little more science to sales, bottom-line improvements of up to 15 percent and top-line sales growth of 30 to 50 percent are easily achievable.[60] In most cases a company must write a sales strategy or sales plan for each business unit or segment. This can be done as a part of the marketing mix or as a separate planning tool. The more efforts are put into the sales plan, the better the chances to succeed at the front. This should go as far as training the sales force one on one in role plays of important situations. In phase 7 of the process of marketing strategy, sales management refers to translating the three major sales strategic elements into sales force language. The three key elements of sales management are database management, customer relationship management, and sales controlling.

Database management per definition requires manageable databases. This is a challenge for many companies, even for those with enterprise resource planning systems. For companies without Enterprise Resource Planning (ERP) systems the difficulties are even greater. My experience shows that a smaller $100 million company without ERP system can have up to eighty different and often noncompatible databases. This includes data harvested and updated by sales people on index cards or notebooks. Customers actually want you to collect a certain amount of data and generally get angry if their account history is not updated, or if they recognize that their data is not correct. What we need is efficient information which tells us enough about an account to make the right approach, proposal and close. Philip Kotler[61] proposes to use data to categorize customers into four groups: most profitable customers, most growable customers, most vulnerable customers, and most troubling customers. Database management is the tool to maximize the profit from the customer relationship.

Customer relationship management (CRM) is about treating a customer and not about software tools. Most of the CRM tools are used as an expensive detour to find out what might be learned in a conversation with the customer. CRM technology can only work if the organization is customer centric and lean. It cannot compensate for bad habits, inefficiency, and lack of frontline contacts of management, and ignorance. Especially in business to business environments, CRM tools should be given into the hand of the customer and allow the businesses to manage their relationship with the vendor themselves. By this the burden of data collection and reporting is taken from the sales people, and they are free to focus on the relationship. W Steel, a midsize steel manufacturer in Europe allows its customers to follow an order of hot rolled strip steel online throughout the process; customers can organize all logistics for the batch themselves and even change standard delivery places. The customers also place their orders online and manage their data. This has reduced calls to client services significantly and increased customer satisfaction enormously. Their sales people now have enough time to work on innovative solutions for customers and to focus on value propositions. Basically W Steel relies on information managed by their customers. This is not CRM, but RMC, the relationship managed by the customer.

In sales controlling we do everything that is required to keep the current closing ratio where we want it and to achieve our future sales goals. There are two ways of selling: with a sales force or without a sales force. Selling without a sales force is much more difficult, because you only have passive influence on the customer through the internet or through referrals. This is the reason why most companies still use some kind of sales force. More and more organizations however rely on contract sales people instead of hiring sales reps. Contract sales people are very difficult to lead, and I therefore advocate hiring sales people. Payment should be mostly on performance and for a business this means profit, not revenues. Every sales person should have a personal profit and loss account (P&L). A new sales person should be "in the money" after eighteen months, which means that he/she should have a positive result on her P&L. If not, they should be terminated. Payment should be a low fix salary and about two-third or more variable. Commission payments should be made monthly, because sales people need short-term motivation. Transparency is an important motivator, and therefore sales people should measure themselves and report their numbers to the sales manager who may double-check them occasionally. Sales controlling is not a field where financial controlling people should spend time. Measures in sales controlling could be sales call per day, time spent per call, profitability per sales call, closing ratio, account structure, and of course sales person profitability. The more a sales person makes in commissions, the better for the company, if the commission is based on profitability. Top sales people often sell many times more than the average sales person, and I know many cases where they make even more than the CEO.

Phase 8: Implementation

About 70 percent of all strategies are never implemented. The reasons are manifold, but most of the times management is just not committed to a systematic follow through and daily business wash strategic emphasis away. Another frequent problem is that crucial initiatives scheduled to be executed at a later time are eaten up by budget cuts. There is a simple way to avoid stalemate and to ensure that initiatives are executed as planned. Ideas and initiatives arise throughout the process. They need to be collected, documented, and categorized. A good way to do so is an assessment in terms of the four perspectives of the balanced scorecard: customer, financial, internal, learning and growth.[62] All four perspectives need to be defined first. We commonly do this by selecting three to five criteria for each perspective and sometimes we also weight them. Each initiative should then be rated on the four criteria. It makes sense to describe the process in detail in a little manual. The result of the process is a set of three portfolios: market impact, feasibility, and priority. The ratings of customer and financial form the market impact portfolio and the ratings of internal and learning and growth become the feasibility portfolio.

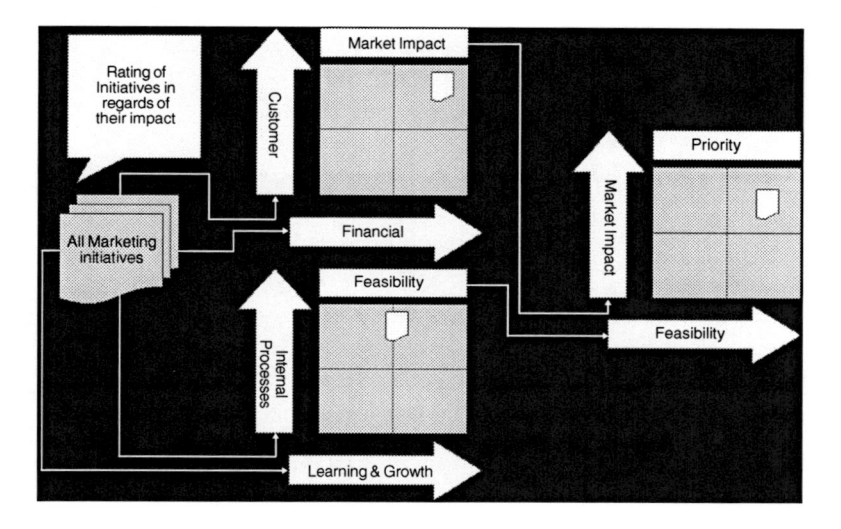

Figure 26: Assessment of Initiatives

The priority portfolio is created by rolling market impact and feasibility over as new axes. The axe values on priority are the total of points from each customer/financial and internal/learning and growth. If an initiative scored seven points on customer and five points on financial, the total would be twelve points, and these would be rolled over onto the market impact axes. The same procedure applies for feasibility, which is the total of internal and learning and growth. The initiatives with the highest position in the priority portfolio get the right of way in resource allocation. Once resources are allocated to an initiative they should not be taken away anymore, even if budgets need to be cut. This is an important principle in implementation of strategies. If cost-cutting measures are required, they should be made on program basis and impact the projects of lower priority. Finally all initiatives should be guided by balanced scorecards that include quantitative and qualitative objectives. Every project needs a project owner and the status report should be a standard item on the agenda of monthly management board meetings.

Customers and Markets			Financials and Reults		
Quantitative Objectives	2004	2007	Quantitative Objectives	2004	2007
• Qualitative Objectives			• Qualitative Objectives		

Structure and Processes			Personnel, Learning and Growth		
Quantitative Objectives	2004	2007	Quantitative Objectives	2004	2007
• Qualitative Objectives			• Qualitative Objectives		

Figure 27: Balanced Scorecard for Initiatives

In their third book in the Balanced Scorecard series, Kaplan and Norton[63] summarize that successful execution of a strategy is an equation with three components: Breakthrough results can only be achieved if a strategy is evident and measurable and if the strategy is executed. This equation results in the simple philosophy that you cannot manage what you cannot measure and that you cannot measure what you cannot describe.

CHANGE

As soon as you have crafted your strategy and are in full swing of implementation the predictable will happen: A change in environment or an unforeseen opportunity arises, and it forces you to change your strategy. Sometimes you have to abandon it completely; sometimes you have to make up to significant adaptations. This should not be considered exceptional in any way. Strategies may have a pretty short shelf life. This is one reason why the process of crafting a strategy should be simple and institutionalized. The more time consuming and complex it is, the less adaptive an organization becomes. My consultancy did the strategy process for the freight division of the Swiss Federal Railway system—SBB. SBB is a billion Swiss franc (about seven hundred fifty million dollars) operation. The project started in June 2003 with a three-day training for senior and middle management to bring everyone up to speed in methodology and terms. By August 2003 five market segment workshop series were under way, and with only three sessions per market segment all strategy work was finalized mid of October the same year. The same year SBB freight was out of their losses and resegmented their operations. European deregulation allowed the formerly federal institution to compete for freight outside the Swiss borders. They established hubs in Cologne, Germany, and Genoa, Italy, to create a north-south freight corridor through Europe. Simultaneously the German competitor Railion developed a similar strategy and bought a 20 percent stake in the second Swiss carrier Berne-Loetschberg-Simplon, BLS. The alps are the key to any north-south strategy in European logistics. BLS operates the Loetschberg and Simplon tunnels while SBB operates on the Gotthard route. The whole situation had changed again for SBB and to make it even worse; the extension of the European Union with ten new members in May 2004 was on the horizon. Every one of those events would trigger an organization to change its strategy completely. The modular concept and the thinking in the eight customer focus parameters however made it easy for SBB to adapt situatively and speedily.

Change is a fact in business life. One of the best books about change was written by Spencer Johnson, a medical doctor. The book is called *Who Moved My Cheese?*[64] and it explains the need for change in a dramatic manner. This passage is from the whomovedmycheese.com Web site:

> The story of "Who Moved My Cheese?" is a simple parable that can be interpreted as you wish, depending on where you feel you are—at work or in your life. In this story, four characters—who represent parts of ourselves—live in a "Maze" and look for "Cheese" to nourish them and make them happy. Two are mice named "Sniff" and "Scurry," and two are little people named "Hem" and "Haw," who are the size of mice but look and act a lot like some people. "Cheese" is a metaphor for whatever you want to have in life—job, relationship, health, peace of mind. And the "Maze" is where you look for it. The story shows what happens to the characters one day, when the Cheese has been moved to another part of the maze. Some are prepared for it and do well; others are surprised and have a difficult time. As you watch what they do, you may see a part of yourself. When Haw is finally able to see what he is doing and laughs at himself, he moves on and finds "New Cheese" while Hem remains hemmed in by his comfort and fears and is left behind. As Haw progresses through the Maze, he writes on the walls what he has learned about change, hoping his

friend Hem will find his way. The story ends with Hem realizing that when you can read the "Handwriting on the Wall," you can do well in changing times.

Whenever I have people in my clientele resisting the changes required to succeed in strategy, I give them a copy of this little masterpiece of philosophy and hope they will learn the following:

- Change Happens: They keep moving the cheese
- Anticipate Change: Get ready for the cheese to move
- Monitor Change: Smell the cheese often so you know when it is getting old
- Adapt to Change Quickly: The quicker you let go of old cheese, the sooner you can enjoy new cheese
- Change: Move with the cheese
- Enjoy Change: Savor the adventure and enjoy the taste of new cheese
- Be Ready to Change Quickly and Enjoy It Again and Again

If these simple messages are obeyed in an organization, it is consequently developing a much stronger overall capability to shape or adapt whenever necessary. If an organization masters the messages, it will be able to lead the revolutions in business[65] and to reimagine itself. If a strategy does not work, just change it. Try again. As Winston Churchill put it, "Success is the ability to go from one failure to another with no loss of enthusiasm." There is no perpetuity in business. In 1994 Jim Collins and Jerry Porras wrote one of the biggest business best-sellers ever: *Built to Last*.[66] In their breakthrough work they compare IBM against Hewlett Packard and Texas Instruments and they focus on the "heavy" part in information technology, i.e., servers and mainframes. Neither Dell nor Compaq are mentioned in the book. You know that the computer world today looks different than the world of Collins and Porras in the early nineties. IBM and HP are different companies today and certainly had enough resilience to adapt. Texas Instruments underwent the most significant change from consumer exposure to business to business. Not calculators, but power management tools, semiconductors, and radio frequency identification (RFid) technology dominate today. The vision of TI is simple: *TI has set a vision to become a premier electronics company providing world leadership in digital solutions for the networked society—a society transformed by personalized electronics, all speaking the same digital language, all able to communicate anytime, anywhere.*[67] By focusing on leadership in revolutionary technologies like RFid, TI again sets the foundation to change itself significantly. RFid labeled goods just became the standard, because Wal-Mart mandated its suppliers to equip all goods with the technology by 2005. The passive energy used in the technology allows it to track basically everything on a worldwide basis. I just read about an idea to let kids wear bracelets with RFid to trace them. Imagine what relief this could provide for parents who do not know where their kids are (the idea could be scary too on the other hand). It is not technology that turns TI into a great enterprise; it is their ability to shape the company toward new directions quickly that makes TI exceptional. Collins followed up on his first book with a five-year study about long-term superiority of companies that was published six years later.[68] Here he says that technology alone is not a key point to becoming great, the point is how a company reacts to technological change and how an organization turns unrealized potential into results. These findings are backed by a recent article about resilience in the *Harvard Business Revue*[69] which says that success has become a very fragile issue. Organizations do not change fast enough because they believe that they do not have to change. The *Titanic* would never have sunk if the crew had been aware of the vulnerability of the ship. But the vessel was perceived unsinkable, so why would you believe it could sink even if an iceberg hit its hull. The crew followed procedures to deal with the accident that were based on having an unsinkable ship. If they had been resilient, they would have assessed the situation more quickly, and they could have saved the ship with a zero-based approach. This is what is needed in turbulent times. To make the future, an organization cannot depend on the past. An inventory of today's best practices does not necessarily conform to the skills required for the future. Resilient organizations are able to handle a number of challenges. First, they must become entirely free of nostalgia and arrogance to openly assess situations and to evaluate the need for change. Secondly, they have to develop an ability to create enough new options as alternative to dying strategies. Thirdly, they need an ability to divert resources from yesterday's products and programs to tomorrow's. This includes the support of a broad portfolio of breakout experiments with the necessary capital and talent. Fourthly, they must embrace a creed that extends beyond operational excellence and flawless execution, they must be able to abandon incumbent business models and develop revolutionary business concepts. In my practice I identified two drivers for resistance to change: tradition and location. The more traditional an organization is, the greater the difficulty to deal with change. I call this also the Titanic Effect. This effect has five phases: euphoria, trance, winning team, catastrophe, and no rescue. The ship was faster, bigger, safer than any other ship and it had a renowned skipper. Everyone was euphoric. Indicators of euphoria in organizations are remarks that because we work better, we are more innovative, we have better skills, and mistakes others made cannot happen in our organization.

The atmosphere on board was luxurious, carefree, and everybody trusted on technology and on progress. Trance can be recognized when everybody is convinced that they are going to reach their goals without mishaps, and everything critical is faded out. Short before the catastrophe is the winning team phase. Early warnings are ignored, and the alerters are rebuked because they jeopardize the operation. Whoever does not join and support the big departure is called a waverer, preventer, weakling, or even a traitor. Then the unthinkable happens. The reactions are disbelief, paralysis, covering up. Others triumph in claiming that they always knew. What must not be will not be realized. Rescue becomes a second catastrophe because measures are inadequate, rash, and late, without concept or orientation. Because the catastrophe was considered impossible, not enough life boats were on board the *Titanic*. Location is the second driver to resistance to change. Tom Peters cites Orson Welles as Harry Lime in the *Third Man*[70]: "In Italy for 30 years under the Borgias they had warfare, terror, murder, bloodshed—and produced Michelangelo, Leonardo Da Vinci, and the Renaissance. In Switzerland they had brotherly love, 500 years of democracy and peace—and what did they produce? The cuckoo clock." Of course this quote is a little bit bold, but it somehow hits the nail (I can say this because I was raised in Switzerland). The more dynamic and the more pressure people are exposed to, the more they tend to change and to become resilient. This is one reason why America is one of the best places for entrepreneurs. It does not matter how many times you fail, it matters what you accomplish the one time you do not fail. And if you become rich, good for you! On the other hand, if you go bankrupt in Europe, you are out of society, because Europeans just do not move to another state and start over again. Failure sticks to those who failed. This is the reason why many of the successful Europeans do not live in Europe anymore. They prefer the Americas, or Asia-Pacific, because here you have to be flexible and resilient to make it. Location influences resilience. Estonia in the Baltics has one of the highest percentages of entrepreneurs and the youngest government in the world (average age is twenty nine). The country is too small to host large companies, so people had to reinvent their location and come up with revolutionary concepts. They boldly introduced Internet and wireless technology all over the country and became a technology and financial power house. Basically something Switzerland could have done, if it would have had more resilience. Companies in locations with more flexible and of course tougher business environments are forced to change more frequently and therefore are more resilient. The labor laws in these areas also tend to be more supportive for change. A Swiss company that went through the *Titanic* syndrome and reinvented itself is Asea Brown Boveri, or ABB. In a strategic move that turned out to be a catastrophe, ABB sold off its core business in turbine and power plant technology. It was forced to reimagine what it could do. Today they are again in leading positions in their three business segments: power technology, automation technology, and petrochemicals. Long-time rival Alstom did not recognize the need to be flexible and nearly collapsed in May 2004. It only survived after reaching a financial restructuring and recapitalization agreement with their banks end of May 2004. Merriam-Webster tells us that "change implies making either an essential difference often amounting to a loss of original identity, or a substitution of one thing for another."[71] Enjoy change—a lot!

ONE-PAGE SUMMARY

Eight driving forces for success in business:

1. Decide with what kind of products and services (1. Wow)
2. How much money are you going to make (2. EVA)
3. In what kind of business environment (3. Residual Uncertainty)
4. And with what kind of priority (4. Shoot)
5. Evaluate how to design customer-oriented business processes (5. ETBW)
6. How to market your products to the target segments (6. Top of Mind)
7. Master the process to translate concepts into market share (7. Just do It).
8. Accept that you will only succeed if you are aware of the constant need to change and the quest for resilience (8. Change)

INDEX

Symbols

20/20 foresight; twenty override 33
3Com Corporation; three override 24, 44
80/20 Principle, The (Koch); eight override 31
80/20 principle; eight override 31, 34

A

ABB (Asea Brown Boveri, Ltd.) 54, 100
acid test; acid override 33
Agenda, The (Hammer) 57
Airbus 36
ALDI (Albrecht and Dieter) 35
Allen, Woody 25
Alstom 100
Amazon 26, 49
Andy Grove Perspective 75
Ansoff, Igor 80
AOL (America Online, Inc.) 24
Apple 35
Associated Press 40
AT&T (American Telephone & Telegraph) 50

B

Bain, Alexander 40
Balanced Scorecard, The (Kaplan and Norton) 94
Bank of America 60, 88
bargaining power 79
Bauknecht 54
Baumann, Willy 25
Bayer 36
Belin, Edouard 40
Belinograph 40
Bhote, Keki 14
 Ultimate Six Sigma, The 14
Big Blue 60
Bill Gates Perspective 75
Bleicher, Knut 43
BLS (Berne-Loetschberg-Simplon) 96
Boeing 36
Borden, Neil H. 84

Bossidy, Larry 66
Branson, Richard 10, 13, 66
Brin, Sergey 31
Built to Last (Collins and Porras) 97
business administration 10, 31
business field 47

C

Cargo Domino 42
Caselli, Giovanni 40
ceoexpress.com 71
Champy, James 16
  X-Engineering the Corporation 16
chaos theory 45
Churchill, Winston 97
Cialis 36
Cingular 50
Circle of Innovation, The (Peters) 30
Clarkson, Max 89
  metaprinciples 90
Coase, Ronald 25, 45
Collins, Jim 97
  Built to Last 97
Comcast 24
communication 18
competitive advantage 24
Competitive Advantage (Porter) 24
confusograms 9
Courtney, Hugh 33, 37
  20/20 foresight 33
  strategy development
    levels of uncertainty 38
CRM (Customer Relationship
    Management) 91
customer ranking 67

D

Danzas 20
Dell Computers 10
Dell, Michael 10
Delta Airlines 57

demand curve 13
Deutsche Post 20
Deutsche Telekom 50
DHL (Dalsey, Hillblom, and Lynn)
    20
Diebold 68
differentiation 22
differentiation focus 25
Disneyland Resort Paris 28
diversification 80
Drucker, Peter 27

E

Earthlink 63
eBay 22, 26
Edwards Air Force Base 75
Ehrbar, Al 26
Einstein, Albert 31
Embraer and Bombardier 36
Encorus 37
Enron 26
eONE Global 37
ETBW (Easy to Do Business With)
    56
  the challenge 59
Ethernet protocol 25, 44
EuroExpress 20
EVA (Economic Value Added) 29

F

FedEx 17
findwhat.com 46
First Data 37
fish tank phenomenon; fish override
    31, 46
Fleet Boston 88
flock of bird phenomenon; flock
    override 46
Florida Gulf Course University 52
Ford 47
formulating market strategies 94

crafting the strategy 84
implementation 94
market analysis 75
marketing mix 90
portfolio management 77
sales management 92

G

Gandhi, Mohandas 30
GE (General Electric) 16, 54
Gillette 81
Gladiator 28
Glaxo Smith Kline 36
GM (General Motors) 47
Godin, Seth 21
Google 31
googol; googol override 31
Gove, Andy 75
GPS (Global Positioning System) 31
Gray, Elisha 40
Greyhound 48
GSM (Global System for Mobile Communication) 37

H

Hammer, Michael 57
Agenda, The 57
Harley Davidson 71
Harvard Business Revue 80, 98
Harvard University 71
Hewlett Packard 97
Hitachi 60

I

IBM (International Business Machines) 32, 97
inside in approach; inside override 39
integration 51
ISP (Internet Service Provider) 24
IT partnership 84

J

Johnson, Spencer 96
Who Moved My Cheese? 96
Jordan, Michael 68

K

Kaplan, Robert S.
 Balanced Scorecard, The 94
Kearney, A. T. 64
Kinkos 17
kinkos.com 17
Koch, Richard 31
Korn, Arthur 40
 telephotography 40
Kotler, Philip 84
 Marketing Management 84
Kummer, Madeleine 12

L

LDX (Long Distance Xerography) 40
Leadership Primer, A (Powell) 32
Levitra 36
Lewis, Peter 58
licensure 51
Lilly ICOS 36

M

M-commerce (Mobile Telephone Commerce) 37
Magnafax Telecopier 40
market development 80
marketing 54
Marketing Management (Kotler) 84
marketing mix 47, 84, 90
marketing power 79
McIntosh 35
McKinsey & Company 61, 76
Merriam-Webster 100
Metcalfe, Robert 24, 44

3Com Corporation 44
  Ethernet protocol 44
  Metcalfes law 44
Metcalfes law 44
Microsoft 35
Mitsubishi Motors 86
moment product curve 13
Moore, Gordon 44
  Moores law 44
Moores law 44
Motorola 37
  Iridium satellite phone system 37
MSN (Microsoft Network) 63
Murphy, Edward A. 75
Murphy's law 75

N

NASDAQ (National Association of Securities Dealers Automated Quotation System.)
  utomated Quotation System.) 46
Needle Destroyer 41
net promoters 62
Nextel 50
Nike 68
NOPAT (Net Operating Profits After Taxes) 27
Norton, David P.
  Balanced Scorecard, The 94

O

OEM (Original Equipment Manufacturers) 54
one-page strategy 84
Only the Paranoid Survive (Grove) 75
OnStar 21
orchestration 51
outperformance 9
outside in approach; outside override 42

P

Page, Larry 31
Pajero 86
Palace Hotel 14
pantelegraph; pant override 40
Parallel Intel 24
Pareto, Vilfredo 31
Pebble Beach Golf Club 14
Pendt 25
Personal Valet 28
Peters, Tom 11, 12, 21, 99
  Circle of Innovation, The 30
  Pursuit of Wow!, The 11
Pfizer 35
Plattner, Hasso 10
Porras, Jerry 97
  Built to Last 97
Porter, Michael 23, 24, 43, 72
  Competitive Advantage 23
  positioning 82
Powell, Colin 32
  Leadership Primer, A 32
pricing 87
  competitive 87
  cost based 86
  enhanced 87
  value based 87
principle of least effort (Zipf); principle override 32
product / market mix 81
product development 80
product power 78, 79
product-centered business 14
Progressive 58
Pursuit of Wow!, The (Peters) 11

R

Railion 96
RE/MAX Real Estate Consultants 87
red hot 14

red hot curve 14
Reichhelt, Fredrick 62
relationship organization 55
Reynolds, Craig 45
  flock of bird phenomenon 45
RFid (Radio Frequency Identification) 98
Richard, Koch
  80/20 Principle, The 31
Ries and Traut 86
RMC (Relationship Managed by Customers) 92
Rolex 13

S

sales management 90, 92
  customer relationship management 92
  database management 91
  sales controlling 92
SAP (Systems, Applications, and Products in Data Processing) cessing) 10
SBB (Schweizerische Bundesbahnen) 95
scale focus 25
segment power 79
service-centered business 16
Servisco 20
SIP (Strategic Inflection Point) 75
Sirotta, Milton 31
SMS (Short Message Service) 38
Sony Play Station 2 14
Southwest Airlines 63
Sprint 44, 50
  PCS Network 44
St. Gallen Management Model 43, 44
stake 88
stakeholders 90
  consumer 88
  core 88
  employee 88
  environmental 88
  owner 88
  primary 88
  secondary 88
  strategic 88
Starbucks Coffee 61
Steinmetz, Charles Proteus 16
Stern Stewart & Company 26
Straight from the Gut (Welch) 33
strategic control point 12
strategic positioning 81
Sun Microsystems, Inc 60
Swiss Federal Freight Railway 42
Swissair 61
SWOT Matrix (Strengths, Weaknesses, Opportunities, Threats hreats) 77

T

T-Mobile 50
telephotography 40
Texas Insruments 97
Third Man 99
TietoEnator 84
time to market;time override 26
Time Warner 24
Titanic Effect 99
top of mind 67
  levels 62
  emotional 61
  geographical 61
  image 61
  presence 61
transaction costs 25, 45
transparency 92
Turner, Ted 24

U

Ultimate Six Sigma, The (Bhote) 14
UMTS (Universal Mobile Telecommunication System) 37
University of Phoenix 52

USGAAP (United States Generally Accepted Accounting Principles)
Principles) 49
USP (Unique Selling proposition) 31

V

Verizon 24, 50
Viagra 35
Virgin Atlantic Airways 10, 66, 71
Virgin Mobile 44
VoiceStream 50

W

W Steel 91
Wachovia 88
Wal-Mart 98
Wall Street Journal Europe 49
Walt Disney Corporation 28
Walter W. (founder of the company that invented Needle Destroyer)
  le Destroyer) 42
Welch, Jack 49
Welles, Orson 99
Western Electric Company 40
Western Union 37
Whirlpool Corporation 28, 54
Who Moved My Cheese? (Johnson) 96
whomovedmycheese.com 96
Wi-Fi (wireless fidelity) 24, 37
Wilsdorf, Hans 13
  Rolex 13
Worldcom 26
wow business; wow override 22
  wow products 15
  wow service 19

X

X-Engineering the Corporation (Champy) 16
Xerox Corporation 40
  LDX (Long Distance Xerography) 40
  Magnafax Telecopier 40

Z

Zipf, George K. 31
  principle of least effort 31

ENDNOTES

Chapter 1
1. Tom Peters, *The Pursuit of Wow!* (New York: Vintage Books, 1994).
2. Swiss International Airlines was established April 1, 2002.
3. Keki R. Bhote, *The Power of Ultimate Six Sigma* (New York: AMACOM, 2003).
4. James Champy, *X-Engineering the Corporation: Reinventing Your Business in the Digital Age* (New York: Warner Books, 2002).
5. Keki R. Bhote, *The Ultimate Six Sigma: Beyond Quality Excellence.*
6. www.servisco.pl.
7. www.onstar.com.
8. Tom Peters, *Re-imagine* (New York: Dorling Kindersley, 2003).
9. Seth Godin, *Purple Cow* (New York: Penguin Books, 2003).

Chapter 2
10. Michael Porter, *Competitive Advantage: Creating and Sustaining Superior Performance* (New York: Free Press, 1998).
11. Ronald H. Coase, *The Nature of the Firm*, (Economica, 1937).
12. Al Ehrbar, *EVA: The Real Key to Creating Wealth* (New York: Wiley, 1998).
13. Peter Drucker, "The Theory of Business," *Harvard Business Review* (1994).

Chapter 3

14. Encarta.msn.com, Keyword Mohandas Karachmand Ghandi, reference to the Amritsar Massacre.
15. Tom Peters, *The Circle of Innovation* (New York: Knopf, 1997).
16. www.google.com/corporate.
17. Richard Koch, *The 80/20 Principle* (New York: Currency Doubleday, 1998).
18. Colin Powell, *Leadership Primer*, see also Oren Harari, *The Leadership Secrets of Colin Powell* (New York: McGraw-Hill, 2002).
19. Jack Welch, *Jack: Straight from the Gut* (New York: Warner Books, 2001).
20. Hugh Courtney, *20/20 Foresight* (Boston: Harvard Business School Press, 2001).
21. www.aldifoods.com.

Chapter 4

22. www.encorus.com.
23. Stuart Van Aucken, The Challenge of Marketing, Lecture SGMI E-Learning FGCU 2002.
24. www.ideafinder.com.
25. Name changed.
26. www.sbbcargo.ch.
27. Hans Ulrich, "St. Galler Management Model" (Bern, 1974).
28. Michael Porter, *Competitive Strategy* (New York: Free Press, 1980).
29. Knut Bleicher, *Das Konzept integriertes Management* (Frankfurt: Campus, 1999).
30. www.virginmobileusa.com.
31. Craig W. Reynolds, "Flocks, Herds, and Schools: A Distributed Behavioral Model" (Anaheim, Computer Graphics, 21(4), 1987, pp. 25-34).
32. Wall Street Journal Europe, Oct. 16, 2002, pages A1/A6.
33. Jack Welch, "Straight from the gut," p. 343f.
34. www.fgcu.edu/cob.

Chapter 5

35. Michael Hammer, *The Agenda* (New York: Crown Business, 2001).
36. Tom Peters, *Re-imagine* (New York: Dorling Kindersley, 2003).

Chapter 6

37 Swissair was a McKinsey account.
38 Fredrick F. Reichheld, "The Number One You Need to Grow," *Harvard Business Review* (12/03).
39 A.T. Kearney, *Your Customer Your Boss* (Publication 2001).
40 Larry Bossidy, Ram Charan, *Execution: The Discipline of Getting Things Done* (New York: Crown Business, 2002).

Chapter 7

41 Nike, Michael Jordan Poster of 1998.
42 Bossidy, Charan, *Execution*.
43 www.ceoexpress.com.
44 Peters, *Re-imagine*, p. 116.
45 Porter, *Competitive Strategy*.
46 Chris Stern, "SWOT: An Applied Methodology on How to Use Strengths, Weaknesses, Opportunities, and Threats" (U.S. copyright TX 5-672-433, 1/17/2003).
47 Andrew S. Grove, *Only the Paranoid Survive* (New York: Currency Books, 1996).
48 www.murphys-law.com, article from "The Desert Wings" (March 3, 1978).
49 www.yr.com, "Brand Asset Valuator."
50 James D. Lenskold, *Marketing ROI* (New York: McGraw-Hill, 2003).
51 H. Igor Ansoff, *New Corporate Strategy* (New York: Wiley, 1988).
52 www.tietoenator.com.
53 Neil H. Borden, "The Concept of the Marketing Mix," *Journal of Advertising Research* (June 1964), pp. 197-208.
54 Philip Kotler, *Marketing Management* (New York: Prentice Hall, 1999—10th ed).
55 Al Ries, Jack Traut, *Positioning* (New York: McGraw-Hill, 2000).
56 www.pajero.com.
57 www.remax.com/inside.
58 IFEM study of Southwest Florida banking habits, May 2000.
59 Max Clarkson "Principles of Stakeholder Management," four conferences hosted by the Centre for Corporate Social Performance and Ethics in the Faculty of Management [now called the Clarkson Centre for Business Ethics and Board Effectiveness or CC(BE)] between 1993 and 1998.

60 Thimothy Lukes, Jennifer Stanley, "Bringing Science to Sales," *McKinsey Quarterly* (2004), Number 3.
61 Philip Kotler, *Marketing Insights From A to Z* (Hoboken: John Wiley & Sons, 2003).
62 Robert Kaplan, David Norton, *The Strategy-Focused Organization: How Balanced Scorecard Companies Thrive in the New Business Environment* (Boston: Harvard Business School Press, 2001).
63 Robert S. Kaplan, David P. Norton, *Strategy Maps* (Boston: Harvard Business School Publishing, 2004).

Chapter 8

64 Spencer Johnson, *Who Moved My Cheese? An Amazing Way to Deal with Change in Your Work and in Your Life* (New York: Putnam's Sons, 1998).
65 Gary Hamel, *Leading the Revolution* (Boston: Harvard Business Publishing, 2000).
66 James Collins, Jerry Porras, *Built to Last* (New York: Harper Business, 1994).
67 http://www.ti.com/corp/docs/company/vision.shtml.
68 Jim Collins, *Good to Great* (New York: Harper Collins, 2001).
69 Gary Hamel, Liisa Välikangas, "The Quest for Resilience," *Harvard Business Revue* (September 2003).
70 Tom Peters, *Re-imagine,* p. 33.
71 Merriam-Webster Collegiate Dictionary.